AN IMMACULATE MISTAKE

An Immaculate Mistake

scenes from childhood and beyond

PAUL BAILEY

BLOOMSBURY

First published 1990
Copyright © 1990 by Paul Bailey

The moral right of the author has been asserted

Bloomsbury Publishing Ltd, 2 Soho Square, London W1V 5DE

A CIP catalogue record for this book is
available from the British Library

ISBN 0 7475 0630 2

10 9 8 7 6 5 4 3 2 1

Photoset by Rowland Phototypesetting Ltd,
Bury St Edmunds, Suffolk
Printed and bound in Great Britain by
Butler and Tanner Ltd, Frome and London

Paul Bailey's unusual, highly eloquent memoir is set for the most part in London in the 1940s and 1950s. The son of a roadsweeper ('If people ask you what your father does for a living, tell them he works for the council,' was his mother's firm injunction) and a domestic help to the rich and famous, he was nicknamed The Professor by his family, who considered that he had 'more brains than were good for him'. As a result of acting triumphs at school, he was obsessed for years with the ambition of becoming a great Shakespearian actor, and was determined to play Hamlet and Richard II before dying young. In his teens, he realized that he was the 'Oscar Wilde type' or a 'pansy', inducing in him feelings of confusion and shame which stayed with him until his early twenties. *An Immaculate Mistake* is composed of scenes or fragments of memory, and dispenses with the ordered narrative of most autobiographies in order to arrive nearer to the truth about the author's past.

For Liz Calder, and
in Jane's dear memory

I was born in February, 1937, in Battersea, south London, the third and last child of Arthur Oswald Bailey and his wife, Helen Maud. He was fifty-four years old, and she was forty-one. He was employed as a roadsweeper, she as a domestic help. They had me christened Peter Harry. Such are the plain facts.

'He who is not very strong in memory should not meddle with lying': these scenes from childhood and beyond were written with Montaigne's caution in mind.

In Error

'You were our mistake,' said my mother. 'You ought not to be here, by rights.'

She was old now, and letting go of her secrets. This one, she knew, would be of particular interest to me.

'We didn't plan to have you, is what I'm saying. People like us had to be very careful when it came to having children. You took me by surprise, and your poor father, too. That was typical of you – determined to be different even before you were born.

On the night of my conception, in May 1936, my parents thoroughly enjoyed their love-making. 'We had no fear of the consequences, because we didn't think there'd be any. A few weeks later, we found out we were wrong.'

I asked her to tell me why they had had no fear.

Well, it was her body, and what had been happening to it lately – that was the reason why they had been able to enjoy themselves. At forty, soon to be forty-one, she was certain that the change had come upon her a little bit earlier than expected. It did with some women. All the signs were there – the hot flushes, the horrible black moods that had no cause she could see, plus the fact that her monthlies – if I understood her meaning – had stopped. With evidence like this, there seemed no need – as there always had in the past – for caution.

'Which we threw to the winds, I have to say.'

This revelation, made when she was eighty-four, did not upset me. She had guessed that it wouldn't, and that I might even be amused by it. I was 'old enough and ugly enough' to face the truth.

Walking home that afternoon, I hesitated for a moment on Albert Bridge and looked down at the water that hadn't claimed me, as I had once assured her it would. Two phrases from childhood came back to me while I stood there: my own 'I wish I'd never been born', which I must have said on the Sunday of the gas oven, and my mother's 'Giving birth to you was the worst day's work I ever did'. I could smile at them now, those expressions of unhappiness and exasperation, in the light of the awareness of my accidental entrance into life.

I was pleased, warmed, by this new knowledge. I could say, as Gloucester says of his bastard son Edmund, that I had come 'something saucily to the world' and that 'there was good sport at (my) making'. Why should it matter to me that I had not been planned? 'You were *our* mistake,' she had said – not *a* mistake. She had chosen the word with care, with affection, I realized.

Then I walked on, thanking my father and mother for the error of their loving ways on a late spring night of thorough enjoyment.

CONFETTI

There had been a wedding at the church that morning. I wanted to pick up and scatter the confetti that lay outside, but my mother pulled me on, eager to get to the shops before the few miserable things worth buying vanished into other women's bags. It was a Saturday in June, and the sunlit street was crowded.

Then the crowd dispersed, in the familiar manner of wartime. The siren had sounded, alerting everyone to the prospect of an air raid. It was necessary to take cover, quickly. Some friends of friends lived near by, and it was to their house my mother decided to go, in the hope of finding them in. I remember how she knocked and knocked at their door, how she shouted our names through the letter-box, how afraid she was that the couple was somewhere else. 'Oh, thank God,' she said when she at last heard footsteps, and a voice advising her to keep her hair on.

My mother apologized to the man who let us in. She was sorry for the inconvenience. 'It's the Germans who should be sorry, not you,' he responded, leading us through the kitchen to the back yard, where the concrete shelter had been built. His wife was already inside. She had tried to make it as homely as she could, she explained. With their favourite ornaments and family photographs for decoration, and a strip of carpet on the floor, it looked less dark and dreary, less like what it really was. We were invited to sit down – a chair for my mother, a cushion for me – and to wait until the All Clear went.

('You had your nose in a book all the while that raid was going on,' my mother told me, years later. 'I swear you didn't hear a single bang. If Hitler himself had come goosestepping into that shelter, you wouldn't have noticed him.')

When the raid was over, my mother thanked the friends of friends for protecting us, and declined their offer of tea – she had to rush back to her husband, who would be as worried about her as she was worried about him.

We returned to the sunshine, and to a street that had changed. I saw, beyond the smoke and dust, that the church had gone, and that the confetti I'd wanted to play with was buried under broken stone and shattered glass, entirely out of sight.

*

The second bomb – we called it the 'doodlebug' – that destroyed the Railway Tavern damaged the house where I was born as well: it was declared unsafe and we were ordered to leave. In another of the neighbouring houses affected by the blast, a small boy died strangely. When the explosion occurred in the middle of the night, the pillow on which his head was resting burst open and he was suffocated by the feathers flying out of it.

My mother took me off to the tiny house in a Hampshire village where my grandmother had given birth to five daughters and four sons. (These were the living, but it was hinted that there had been others who had come into the world for a mere matter of hours or days. And there might have been more children if my grandfather had not been killed in an accident at the tanning factory, at the age of forty-six.) 'You should count yourself lucky you're staying with the family. Most London kiddies are sent off to complete strangers, and God only knows what happens to them after that. You hear some terrible stories.'

'What stories, Mum?'

'Never you mind what stories.'

'Tell me,' I implored her. 'Tell me.'

'There's stories,' she pronounced, 'and then there's stories. And that's my last word on the subject.'

('There's doctors, and then there's doctors'; 'There's books, and then there's books'; 'There's women, and then there's women' – she used this adaptable phrase to differentiate between the respectable and the dissolute, the worthy

7

and the unworthy, the good and the bad. Once, praising the Cox's Orange Pippin, she observed, 'There's apples, and then there's apples.' As a child, I was irritated by these pronouncements, for they left too much unsaid: 'There's war, and then there's war' seeming peculiarly inadequate.)

Travelling to the country was not a simple business for my mother. If the train departed at eleven in the morning, she insisted on our being at the station by nine. 'You'd think you were going to Timbuctoo, to judge by the fret you're in,' my father would complain. 'Calm yourself, woman.'

'It's the way I am. I can't help it.'

During the inevitable two hours of waiting, she wondered aloud if she had remembered to write to her mother to say we were coming – 'She'll have our guts for garters, otherwise' – and mentioned the items she imagined she had forgotten to pack.

I suggested, once, that she open the suitcase and look inside. Then she would know exactly what was missing.

'And have people peering at our belongings? I should think not.'

After my father's death, she became even more fretful on journeys. She had the gas to worry about now. 'If your dad was still alive, he'd soon smell it escaping and turn it off.' Her Gas Moment, as I named it, came when the train, or coach, in which we had been among the first to seat ourselves, started moving. 'I've left the gas on,' she whispered. 'No, you haven't,' I assured her. 'How would you know? You never see what's in front of you.' It was pointless to argue. There would be a telegram waiting for her at the other end, with the news that our house and everything we owned, not to mention the family who lived downstairs, had been blown to bits. I advised her to pull the communication cord and stop the train. 'Don't be so wicked,' she scolded. Wicked? 'Think of the people who'd be missing their connections and having their Christmas holidays ruined. It's a wicked idea.'

'The country' in my childhood meant either Hampshire or Sussex, and it was the latter I preferred. I had more freedom there, with no stern grandmother to reprimand me. My Uncle Bill was the head gardener on the large estate at Herstmonceux Castle and I and my cousins played on the lawns while he worked.

One post-war summer afternoon, when my uncle had gone home, they dared me to climb an oak tree. I climbed up and up and up, amazed at my daring and prowess. Then I stopped and looked down, and in an instant felt the keenest terror of my life. I was too frightened to scream. I clung to the branch on which I was perched, and prayed that I wouldn't fall. Descent was impossible now that I had been robbed of the courage I had possessed only minutes earlier. 'Ladder,' I managed to say. 'Get a ladder.' My cousins responded with taunts of 'Cowardy cowardy custard' and ran off, laughing. I remained high in the oak tree until it was almost dark. I cried when my uncle rescued me, from shame as much as relief. Boys, I was told, do not cry. Crying was what little girls did, because it was in their nature.

That was my cousins' single act of cruelty, as inexplicable today as it was then. Both girls abetted me when I pretended to be my twin brother, who did not exist. Of all the games I played as a boy, this was the one I enjoyed most. It was fun being someone else, escaping from the Peter that I was into the Paul of my imagination, giving him different characteristics, different interests. Paul was a livelier creature than his dull impersonator, it seemed to me. He had to be created afresh, newly imagined, each time I decided to become him.

Another Paul, *Sir* Paul, was talked about in Castle Cottage, the big and beautiful house where my uncle and aunt and their daughters lived. 'Poor Sir Paul' was the phrase I often heard. I did not understand. How could he be poor when he was rich? The castle was his, and the gardens. How was he poor? 'He's poor because he's been unlucky,' was the answer I received. Back in London, I asked my mother why Sir Paul was poor and unlucky. 'That would be telling,' she said. 'It's not a story for young ears.'

(In 1941, Sir Paul Latham, a Conservative Member of Parliament and an officer in the Royal Artillery, was accused of committing an 'improper act' with two gunners. Fearing scandal, he attempted suicide by crashing his motor bike. He survived the crash, but had to have a leg amputated. He was sentenced to two years' imprisonment for misbehaving with the soldiers and for the suicide attempt. The scandal persisted. Yet my uncle never said a derogatory word about his employer, and neither did my mother, who considered Sir Paul a 'true gentleman'. Years later, when she and other members of my family informed me that pansies were the sons of the idle rich, they must have been thinking of 'poor Sir Paul'. The two gunners – from back-street homes, like the Peter who was being educated – were forgotten.)

The three names I associate with those summers in Sussex are not English. My cousins collected signed photographs of film stars, which they obtained by writing to an address in Culver City, California. The smiling likenesses of the famous adorned their bedroom walls. I copied out their regular letter and posted it to America, to Turhan Bey. I wrote to him simply because I loved the sound of 'Turhan Bey'. There was no one called Turhan Bey in Battersea or Herstmonceux or Titchfield, where my grandmother had her domain. Turhan Bey, in desert robes, sent his best to Peter, wishing him everything he wished himself.

My aunt and uncle gave an annual children's party in the garden behind their home. She prepared the food and drink – jellies, jam tarts, trifle, orange and lemon squash – and he supplied the entertainment. Uncle Bill's party piece was to dress up as a woman and sing a slightly risqué song. He was hairy and simian in appearance, the black stubble showing through the make-up he had applied to his weather-beaten face. He sported balloons for breasts, which he always burst at the end of his act: 'Bang goes the left titty, bang goes the right.' One year, he disguised himself, with limited resources, as Carmen Miranda, the film star noted rather for the exotic fruits she carried on her person than for any ability as a singer and dancer. Carmen Miranda bore a pineapple on her head, and used bananas as earrings. In wartime England, my uncle was restricted to apples, pears and cherries.

I, I, I, I, I, I like you very much
I, I, I, I, I, I think you're grand

he sang, swishing his wife's polka-dot frock from side to side. That was all he knew of the song, so he then made a joke about maracas, which only the adults appreciated. He repeated the two lines again and again, and tried to dance the rumba – which wasn't easy for him, in high-heeled shoes – and brought his performance to a close with a protracted fruit striptease: 'You want my cherry? You fancy my pear? How much you pay for my apples?'

The third foreign name is that of a German prisoner-of-war, Matthias Hess, who was dear to my mother's memory. His calm and gentle nature is celebrated in a separate story.

When I think of my grandmother, I think first of snuff, which she inhaled to clear her head. The skin between her nose and upper lip had turned brown from it. Her hands and face and clothes smelled of snuff, and so did the chair she sat in for most of the day, in front of the blackened range on which a kettle was perpetually coming to the boil.

That chair was her throne, from which she ruled over her brood. My father, of whom she disapproved, had refused to bend the knee in her presence and had banished himself from her house when I was very young. She had been cruel to my sister – who suffered, as did my brother, from rheumatic fever – and he had not forgiven her. My grandmother had no tolerance of illness; regarded it, indeed, as a vice, an indulgence, of the weak-minded. She talked of gumption as she took her pinch of snuff. Gumption was what you had inside and prevented you from becoming ill, and snuff kept you 'up to snuff', meaning 'healthy'. Gumption and snuff constituted her own grim panacea.

One of her daughters had married a 'good-for-nothing' and was now 'reaping a just reward' for not being sensible. In the immediate years after the separation from her husband, this least assertive of my aunts was prone to fits. I accompanied her when she went shopping, on my grandmother's orders, in case she had a seizure. I remember the suddenness of the fit I witnessed – how I turned to see her shaking; how I then attempted to hold her upright, and how I slumped to the ground alongside her; how she foamed at the mouth, and how I waited for her agony, and my embarrassment, to be over.

My disgraced aunt was allowed home by her mother on condition that she earn her keep. The ancient tyrant sat on her throne in the room that opened on to the street and issued her daily commands. The grate needed sweeping, and the fire stoking; coal had to be brought in, and wood chopped; there was washing to be done, and clothes to be ironed; the table had to be laid for dinner, tea and supper, and the shutters had to be opened or closed.

(In old age, this aunt – who had long ago stopped having fits – became excessively lazy and extremely fat. She permitted the two sisters with whom she lived to cook for her, to wash and iron her clothes, and to wait on her as she had once waited on their mother. She smiled vaguely when they complained of her indolence and referred to her as Your Ladyship or Lady Muck. I watched in silent admiration as she took her late, sly revenge.)

'I'm fussy about what I eat,' said my grandmother. 'You can clean the range, but I won't have you cooking in it.' My aunt, who had cooked for her husband and children, made light of the insult. 'I wouldn't dream of cooking in it, our Mum,' she answered. 'There's nobody's rabbit pie's as good as yours.'

It was the youngest of my uncles, and his mother's favourite, who was required to perform the nastiest household duty. Twice a month, at least, he emptied the deep tin bucket into which we pissed and shat in the clematis-covered privy at the end of the garden. He would dig a hole beyond the vegetable patch and bury the foul-smelling waste. He had 'special chemicals' to dispose of it, which he shook in before 'sealing the grave'.

The outside lavatory we used in Battersea was paradisaical compared to the one behind my grandmother's house. It had a chain – a slightly temperamental chain – which, when pulled vigorously, flushed the stuff away. In Hampshire, in summer, flies buzzed around me as I sat on the wooden seat above the fetid bucket and heard my 'number twos' go plopping into the thick water. I wiped my bottom on the piece of newspaper I had just been reading to distract me from the unpleasant business below, left the shed and treated my offended nostrils to the scent of roses. In winter, there was no such consolation.

'What I Did In My Holidays' was the subject my classmates and I were asked to write about in September 1946, in my first London school. What I had done in my holidays was to invent a twin brother, who spoke in a different voice although he had my face and wore my clothes. I described Paul's adventures in the grounds of the castle with the village children who thought there were two of me, and how annoyed they became when I explained that they would never see Peter and Paul together, because we didn't get on.

It was Peter, the quieter twin, who conducted the funeral service for his aunt's canary, found dead in its cage one morning. Peter led the procession down the garden path and chose a plot for the grave near the eel pond and prayed to God to grant the little bird peace for ever and ever, Amen.

'Is this true?' enquired the teacher when she handed the essay back to me with the magic numbers 10/10 written in red above the title.

'Yes,' I replied.

'Would you like to read it out to the boys and girls?'

'If you want me to, Miss.'

I stood in her place, at the front of the class, and read aloud my true story of the twin brother and the dead canary.

Our new home was almost identical to our old one, now demolished, at the opposite end of the same street. We lived upstairs in the two-storeyed, terraced house, in four poky rooms, connected by a landing. The view from the front-room window was of other identical houses – 'some clean, and some not so', as my mother was quick to notice – and beyond them the tall chimneys of the gas works and the candle factory. From the back bedroom, I saw railway lines, along which goods trains rumbled at night, and an embankment where dandelions bloomed each spring.

When I started attending my second school, founded by Sir Walter St John in 1700, I became aware of the Battersea that existed before the railways and the factories came in the last decades of Victoria's reign – the pleasant Thames-side village famous for the carrots, melons and asparagus, known as 'Battersea Bundles', its market gardeners produced. Near to the school was an exquisite eighteenth-century church, St Mary's, and nearer still the vicarage, where the

Antarctic explorer, Edward Wilson, had briefly lived. There was Battersea House, filled with Jacobean furniture and precious china and glass. These reminders of a feudal age were a few minutes' walk away from the soot-encrusted industrial buildings that loomed just around the corner of our street.

'There's boys, and then there's boys' – it was the rough ones, who wore no shoes for most of the year, my mother commanded me to keep my distance from. 'They were born making trouble. They started as they intended to go on.'

She considered me delicate and fragile when, in reality, I was the healthiest of her three children. My sister, who spent long periods of her childhood in a succession of hospitals, was encouraged to mollycoddle me after my early bout with death. She dressed me while I casually turned the pages of a picture book. 'Left leg out' meant that I had to raise my left leg so that she could slip a sock on to my foot. 'Book down and arms up' was the last order of the day, signifying that it was time to remove my shirt and undervest and get into my pyjamas. It was a kind of game for us, a ritual. 'You're giving the lad airs, between the pair of you,' warned my father. 'He'll be expecting servants when he grows up, and it'll be his tough luck when they don't come running at his beck and call.'

I played in the street, or in Battersea Park, with the sons

and daughters of those my mother deemed respectable. Yet I envied the rough boys and wished to emulate them. They didn't have to be indoors by six or seven in the evening. They weren't washed and scrubbed until they shone, until they merited the dreaded word 'immaculate'.

In 1938, a giant panda arrived at London Zoo. The following Christmas, the toyshops were full of cuddly little replicas of him. An aunt gave me a panda to join the teddy bear I already owned.

We had a cat who was always having kittens, which always disappeared in the night.

'Where have they gone?' I asked my mother. 'To a better world,' was her answer.

That better world, I found out later, was the Thames, into which my father had thrown sack upon sack of them. He laughed when I called him a murderer.

One day in 1940, my mother – exasperated at the prospect of another litter – said to him, 'It's time we had Fluff doctored. Take her to Mr Wilkinson and have her seen to.'

So Fluff was doctored, and stopped giving birth. I wanted to have Teddy and Panda doctored, too, in case they had babies that my cruel father would throw in the Thames. I took them to Mr Wilkinson's house and told his wife that I would like them both doctored: 'As soon as possible, please.'

She laughed, to my amazement. She went on laughing as she accompanied me home.

'He brought them along to be doctored,' she said to my parents, who joined in her laughter. 'To stop them having children. Isn't it rich? Have you ever heard the like of it?'

On the morning of the day the Anglican church was hit by a German bomb, I learned a strange and lovely word. The pretty bits of coloured paper I wanted to pick up and scatter were called confetti, my mother said. Wedding guests threw it over the bride and bridegroom: 'To wish them luck, I suppose.'

'It's gone, Mum,' I said, in the changed street of smoke and dust.

'Yes, I can see. I hope to God there was no one inside it. The vicar must have heard the warning siren.'

'The confetti's gone, Mum.'

'The confetti?'

'It was here before. I wanted to play with it.'

'You'll lose a lot more than confetti in this life, my son.'

PANDA

In 1941, when I was four, I almost died of diphtheria. I spent several weeks in an isolation hospital, with only my panda for company.

It was impossible to eat anything, because of the false membrane that had formed in my throat. The act of swallowing was so painful that I stubbornly refused to drink whatever the nurses offered, including lemonade. Then, one day, they tempted me with orange juice, freshly squeezed. I liked the look of it. I drank a little, and liked its taste.

That I am alive is thanks, in part, to the desperate skill my mother acquired in order to find oranges – dozens and dozens of oranges – at a time when fruit was both scarce and costly. She exerted all her wits to get them, telling shopkeepers what they could hardly believe – that an orange, just one single precious orange, might help to save her younger son's life.

(I did not discover until after her death that she had given birth to a daughter who had died in infancy. While hunting for oranges in bomb-scarred London, she was already acquainted with the peculiar and lasting grief that comes with the loss of a child. The certain prospect of losing another must have been torture for her.)

My condition worsened. Death now seemed inevitable. My parents kept vigil in a room in the hospital, to which every so often the doctor brought them gloomier news.

'If he gets through the next twenty-four hours, there might be some hope': my mother was never to forget the phrase that signalled the remote possibility of a miracle. 'You were that close,' she said to me in her extreme old age. 'They'd given you up, all of them.'

I recovered, drank more orange juice, and went immediately into a long silence.

'He's gone,' the porter at the gate told my mother, who interpreted the words as meaning 'he's dead'. She was accustomed to hearing and saying that people had 'gone'. What she had feared most had finally happened. My recovery had been nothing but an illusion.

'He's gone to a convalescent home, to get better,' the doctor explained to her, when she asked him why I had died. 'That's what the porter meant. It's a nice place, near the country, in Surrey.'

I had clutched Panda to me that morning, assuming that he would go with me to the nice place in Surrey. 'He has to stay here,' said the sister. 'He's too ill to move. We'll let him out when he's well again.'

*

I remained silent during my convalescence, barely responding to the attentions of the nurses. It was thought that I had lost the power of speech.

Shock, was it? I think it must have been. I think I knew, in some wordless way, that I had been on the verge of extinction. The knowledge was there, secreted in the very young body, that oranges – the oranges I still craved – had aided in its fight for survival.

'You're my mummy,' were the words that ended the silence, spoken in a voice that sounded strange to my mother, for it had no trace of Cockney in it. 'You went into hospital a Cockney,' she told me ten years later, after I had won the Elocution Prize at school, 'and you came out a little gentleman.'

I wept when the time came to go home. I wanted to stay with the nurses, and said so, with all the strength my lungs could summon.

My mother – who had to teach her new 'little gentleman' to walk again – promised to buy me another panda, to replace the one I had left behind.

But Panda was Panda, and not to be replaced. I waited for his return, and often asked when it would happen.

My father told me that Panda had taken my germs from me, out of the kindness of his heart. I must always remember what he had done for his friend.

'Here's a big fat book for you, son. It's by old Charlie Dickens. He hadn't been long gone from the world when I was just a nipper.'

It was a very fat book, the fattest I had ever seen, fatter even than the Bible.

'"That will do for my boy," I said to the woman who was throwing it out. "He'll put it to good use."'

The book my father had rescued for me was *Nicholas Nickleby*. It smelt mouldy, and its pages had turned yellow.

'Don't turn your nose up at it, son. I know it's seen better days, but the words are the same ones Charlie wrote, and that's what matters.'

I placed *Nicholas Nickleby* on the kitchen table, because it was far too heavy to hold. I studied every one of the drawings inside, in the order they appeared – starting with 'Mr Ralph Nickleby's First Visit to his Poor Relations' and ending with 'The Children at their Cousin's Grave'. Mr Ralph Nickleby seemed to be very angry at having to visit his poor relations, who didn't look at all poor to me – the women had on long dresses that weren't torn, and the man was quite smart in his funny coat with the two bits hanging down the back that my father told me were called 'tails'. I didn't think they looked as poor as the gypsies on the other side of the street, who went off to Kent for their holidays to pick hops.

'There's poor, and then there's poor,' said my mother, from the stove. 'If I've told you once, I've told you a thousand times – being poor doesn't mean being scruffy. Don't judge people by the likes of *them*.'

I asked my father if Nicholas was real.

'No, son. He'd be make-believe, wouldn't he? Out of Charlie's head.'

That evening, when supper was over and the dishes washed, my father and I were banished to the front room. He had promised to read to me from the 'dust trap', and my mother wanted to listen to some nice music on the wireless.

He began at the beginning.

' "There once lived, in a – " '

He cleared his throat, and began again.

' "There once lived, in a –" ' He gulped. ' "– in Devonshire, one Mr Godfrey Nickleby . . ." '

(Four years after his death, when I put *Nicholas Nickleby* to the 'good use' he had predicted, I realized why he had cleared his throat, why he had gulped, why he had been embarrassed – it was the word 'sequestered' in the novel's opening sentence: 'There once lived, in a sequestered part of the county of Devonshire, one Mr Godfrey Nickleby . . .' 'Sequestered' was totally foreign to him. He'd never had cause to say 'sequestered'. The sight of it on the page had upset him, briefly; had made him keenly aware of his ignorance. The cough and the gulp were his camouflage for that hated 'sequestered'.)

My mother disapproved of *Nicholas Nickleby*. It was a book with a Past – it had been in other hands, and God alone knew whose hands they were. It was old, and it gave off a nasty smell. Its days, in her view, were numbered.

'I can't think what possessed your father to bring it into the house.'

'He brought it home for me.'

'Then why don't you repay him and read it, instead of leaving it about the place to gather dust?'

'I will read it. One day.'

I was fifteen when the day came. I opened *Nicholas Nickleby*, and closed it shut within the hour.

'I have some good news for you,' I told my mother.

'Your good news is usually my bad. What is it now?'

'You can throw this away.' I handed her the 'dust trap'.

'I shall do no such thing. Your father brought that home for you.'

'I'm going to have to borrow it from the library,' I said, teasing her. Then I explained why. 'There are pages missing. Dozens of them.'

'Your dad was not to know.' The sharpness had left her voice. 'The woman didn't say. He thought it would make you happy. He wasn't to know it wouldn't.'

(Watching *Nicholas Nickleby* in the theatre, in 1980, when I was forty-three, I found myself in tears. I remembered my father giving me the book, I remembered 'sequestered', I remembered rushing off to the library on Lavender Hill to get another, complete, copy, and the joy of finding one on the shelves.)

IMMACULATE

'Just because we're poor,' said my mother, 'that's no reason we shouldn't be clean. I've lived with rich men's dirt long enough to know who's decent and who isn't.'

That cleanliness was next to godliness was, for her, a simple and lasting truth. While there was water in the world, no one need be dirty. She had once noticed a tramp, a real gentleman of the road, stop at a horse trough to wash his face. The sight of him had pleased her. 'Which only goes to show,' she added.

'What does it go to show?'

'It goes to show that if a man like him can be bothered to smarten himself up, then so can you, my son.'

She reminded me of the tramp at the horse trough whenever she thought I was getting slovenly. 'He took more trouble over his appearance than you do. Even he had self-respect.'

It wasn't easy staying clean in our house: we had no bathroom, and the lavatory was in the yard. 'It's time you gave yourself a strip-wash,' my mother would say, filling the kitchen sink with hot water from the kettle. 'Wash everywhere, mind. Back as well as front.'

When I was older, I went to the public baths in the High Street, usually on a Friday evening, in order to be my cleanest for the weekend. An elderly attendant handed me a thin cotton towel and a slice of Lifebuoy soap and told me not to be long: 'You've got no more than ten minutes' worth of flesh on you.'

'Immaculate': that was a difficult word my mother knew, for people had said it so often about her children. 'They look absolutely immaculate.' Immaculacy, she believed, was a state of cleanliness few had attained. 'I hope you were looking immaculate,' she used to say to me when I told her I had been for an important interview, or had met someone famous. 'That's what I always brought you up to be. I don't want you letting me down.'

'Oh, I *think* I was immaculate,' I would tease her. 'As much as I'll ever be.'

This immaculate state could not be achieved with the aid of scented soap. Rosehip and lavender were as the perfumes of Arabia to Lady Macbeth – they didn't get at the dirt, as carbolic soap did. Lifebuoy killed all the nasty germs that settled under the skin, whereas that other scented muck made you smell sweet for a while but did you no proper good in the end. 'A fancy scent covers up a worse stink' was one of her sayings.

You weren't thoroughly clean – that is to say, immaculate – if your shoes were scruffy. Mine shone, thanks to her efforts. 'Can you see your face in them?' she'd ask, and I had to answer yes.

They shine still, because of her. I often think of her when I am polishing my shoes to a shine she would have approved of, and hear her exhorting me to use more elbow grease. She died before grubby sneakers became the last word in fashionable footwear. The sight of them would have distressed her as much as that of the tramp at the horse trough had gladdened her. That poor, and far from immaculate, man in a vanished London had signalled something other than merely being clean to her, and I think it had to do with dignity.

'He's a very nice person . . .' she would observe of a

friend of mine; 'She's a very nice girl . . .' and there would always follow the same three words, '. . . and very clean.'

IN NOVEMBER, 1948

I came home that November afternoon to find my father, in a restless fever, in the bed my mother shared with my sister. I did not sleep with him that night, or ever again.

I was eleven years old, and had been his bedfellow since the changes in first, my sister's body, and then mine, had necessitated a separation of the sexes. We had only two small bedrooms in our little part of the little house.

He sounded angry with the world, in his delirium. I was intrigued, rather than frightened. I wanted to make sense of what he was saying, but the words came out in sudden bursts, a few at a time, and I could not follow their course.

He shouted, often. He cursed his mother-in-law, whom he hated, whom he hated so much when he was well that he never mentioned her name. He said it now – to her face, it seemed. But she was a hundred miles away, in Hampshire, in the house he always refused to enter.

There were other names, unrecognizable to me, and – perhaps – to his wife of twenty years. They belonged, I think, to his comrades in the trenches, many long dead. He'd hinted once, on one of our Sunday walks together, that 'over there' had meant hell for him: 'I hope, he said, 'you'll never get to fight abroad.'

More names, more ghosts. I listened to the roll-call, and was moved by a tone in his voice that was unexpectedly tender. Here was affection rising up, and the expression of it gave his features a brief serenity. I can't remember who the distant recipients of that tenderness were. How could I? It was the calm on him then that struck me.

His rage returned, and with it a name I found strange – exotic, even. It was Esther he berated, Esther he scorned, Esther he hit out at.

'Who's Esther?'

My mother answered by telling me not to ask silly questions, and to go and do my homework.

(Esther, I learned in 1985, some months after my mother's death, was my father's first wife. She had gone to live with another man while he was in Flanders. I owe my existence to her unfaithfulness.)

The doctor, who had diagnosed my father as having a severe chill, acknowledged that pneumonia had set in. An ambulance came, and my father was taken to the local hospital, of which it was said that if you went in with a sore finger you left without a hand.

This happened during the night, while I slept alone, fitfully. In the morning, the other bed was empty. It had been made, with my mother's usual fastidiousness.

I did not need to be told what my brother told me, with much hesitation and embarrassment, on the afternoon of 28 November, when I came home from school. My sister's tears were evidence enough, but I had already gained my knowledge from the ghosts and, especially, the mysterious Esther. I had not been able to concentrate on my studies all that week because of them. They had signified something terrible, and, when I learned that it was death, I was not surprised.

The children of Arthur and Esther attended their father's funeral. They had been born before the First World War, and were now middle aged. Laurence, my half-brother, had a wife with an even more exotic name than Esther. She was called Esmé. 'To think we have an Esmé in the family,' said my mother.

Molly, my half-sister, was a civil servant, and obviously brainy. I was told throughout my childhood that, if there was anyone I took after, it was Molly. She had offered to adopt me, I heard later, to relieve my parents' ever-present financial burden. The offer was declined. What a different life I might have led, in her spacious house, with her brainy husband, among her brainy friends. The Professor, as I was called, who had 'more brains than were good for him', regretted for a time that Molly hadn't whisked him away from the house near the gas works.

The following year, Laurence wrote to my mother to say that Esmé had given birth to a son, whom they had named after me. There were no further letters, and we lost touch with Molly.

The two of us were waiting in line for our Christmas meat in the crowded butcher's when my mother, whose reserve in matters of the heart was fiercely maintained, all of a sudden opened her mouth and howled. What a rare luxury grief afforded her that day: the expression – and in public, too – of her deepest, darkest feelings. The rawness of her misery stunned everyone in the shop to silence.

The howling stopped, and my mother dabbed at her eyes with a handkerchief.

'What a fool I've made of myself,' she said. 'I can't think what came over me.'

HISTORICAL

Other boys' fathers played football or cricket. My father played bowls, occasionally. On Sunday mornings in summer, I would sit by the side of the bowling green in the park while he and his ancient mates slowly propelled the balls across the grass. Sometimes, I was the only child among the onlookers. 'Have you come to cheer your grandad on?' a woman asked me once. I nodded assent.

Other boys' fathers had served in the Second World War, which had recently ended. My father had been in Flanders, in the First. He was an old soldier, a veteran of the trenches, a survivor of Passchendaele. His fighting days had finished thirty years earlier, when my friends' fathers were no more than toddlers. He was, I remember thinking, almost historical.

I watched him undress one night, in the tiny back bedroom we now shared together. The hairs on his body were as white as the hairs on his head. It occurred to me, then, that God – who had white hair and a long white beard – must have white hairs underneath his robes as well. 'Does God have white hairs on his chest, Dad?' The question startled him, for he had assumed I was asleep. 'I expect so, son,' he said eventually. 'Not that anyone's ever had a close look, mind you. But I expect He has.'

My father seemed completely historical to me when he was turned out in his Sunday best. In his three-piece suit, starched wing collar and shiny black boots, he was a man from another age. No other father that I knew had a pocket watch on a chain, but mine had. He would produce it from his waistcoat with a flourish and consult its Roman numerals: 'Time we were homeward bound, son. Your mother will give us both what-for if we're late for dinner.'

In spite of the threat of a what-for, we did not hurry back. He liked to walk at what he called a 'gentleman's pace'. On winter days, he would often stop to 'collect a dewdrop' with the handkerchief he carried for this purpose. He had a runny nose, from which a succession of dewdrops dangled: 'It's a sign of age, the dewdrop. You'll know you're old, son, when you start collecting them.'

My father's life began with the rise of the music hall and closed with its decline. I see him most vividly, in his old-fashioned clothes, at the Grand Theatre, near Clapham Junction, one long-ago Saturday night. My mother – who liked to tell how her father had lifted her on to his shoulders the better to see the hearse bearing Queen Victoria as it arrived in Portsmouth from the Isle of Wight – is by his side, and I am with them, enjoying the performance of a funny woman named Kate Carney, who is singing 'Are We to Part Like This, Bill?' in a voice like a foghorn. Bill has been unfaithful to Kate with 'another', and Kate, who looks as if she could flatten a whole army of Bills with her fist, is throwing down the gauntlet across the footlights:

> Who's it to be –
> 'Er or me?
> Don't be afraid to say.

Kate Carney was in her seventies then. All the singers and comics that night seemed old to me. They belonged – as did their songs and jokes – to the past, and here I was, at the age of ten, vaguely aware that I was seeing them just before they vanished for ever.

Yet it isn't the errant Bill, brought to book by the ferocious Kate, who unites my parents in memory for me. It's a different song that conjures them up – and one I never heard, I think, in their presence. Whenever I hear the record of George Robey and Violet Loraine serenading one another tenderly with 'If You Were the Only Girl in the World', my mother and father come to mind, always, in that same improbable Eden the song describes so sweetly. She is looking at him, and he at her, with love.

My father might have sung 'If You Were the Only Girl in the World' in Flanders, for it was a great favourite with the soldiers in the trenches. His 'only girl' was Esther, who was to 'mar his joy' when he returned to England soon after 'the war to end all wars' was over.

WANDERER

Soon after my father's death, I found that I needed to walk away from home. The disappointment I felt when this new compulsion was frustrated by rain or snow or fog was the keenest I had yet experienced. I cursed the weather for denying me the pleasure I most craved – that of escape.

My serious wandering began one Sunday when I told my mother that I was going for a walk. 'Don't leave the neighbourhood,' she cautioned. 'The dark's still coming down early.' I hadn't thought of leaving the neighbourhood before, but now the prospect of walking beyond Battersea, beyond the familiar, was irresistible. The whole of London awaited me. Even as I planned my first journey of exploration, I promised my mother that I would not go far.

I went as far that February afternoon as my legs would take me, to Hyde Park Corner. It was evening, almost bedtime, when I returned.

'Where on earth have you been?' asked my mother. 'I've been worried sick.'

'Walking.'

'Walking where?'

'Around and about.'

Where I walked on those early fatherless Sundays was my secret, not to be revealed. As the year progressed, and the weather brightened, and the dark came down later and later, I ventured farther – into the deserted City, bereft of its dealers, bankers and clerks; its huge monuments to wealth eerily silent, its ancient churches bolted and barred. In Threadneedle Street, the tall blackened buildings seemed to close in on me, and I knew an absurd fear. How and why I decided that the banks were my enemies and had plans to crush me I cannot remember, but the sight of them induced in me a feeling close to terror. I shrank back from their menacing presence. In St Paul's Cathedral, minutes later, I regained the calmness and common sense that had left me so suddenly and inexplicably. I rested there before the long journey homewards.

'You're wearing out good leather and costing me a fortune,' said my mother as she polished my boots, while I soaked my aching feet in a bowl of hot water. 'I don't suppose you're going to tell me where you've been today.'

'Around and about.'

'I supposed aright. It's the same tune every Sunday. I think I'll have you followed, and then I'll know where's around and where's about. That will put an end to the mystery.'

But the mystery was not to be put to an end, thanks to my stealth and cunning. Whenever I set off on one of my mysterious walks, I always assumed that I was being followed by an amateur detective my mother had hired with the promise of an apple pie or a rice pudding. It was not difficult to lose this shadow (if he or she existed), for my knowledge of London's streets was already thorough. I knew exactly when and how to give the pursuer the slip, by darting down an alley or rushing through a crowded museum, oblivious to its exhibits. My loneliness once secure, I walked on until I came to an unexplored part of the sprawling city, which I could now lay claim to, secretly.

I wandered north, south, west and east. My journeys had no plan, no design, and I had no map to guide me. I relied on instinct alone.

'If a stranger wants a word with you, don't stop and chat,' my mother advised. 'I know I've brought you up to be polite, but not with people who talk to children in the open air.'

During that year or so of compulsive walking, I was never approached by strangers, perhaps because I wore the mad look of a determined solitary. My features did not charm or beguile. It was only when my obsession was over, when I walked again at a steady, natural pace, that adults talked to me.

'It's a Sunday,' said my mother.

I didn't look up from the book I was reading. 'I know it is,' I muttered into the page.

'The weather's nice, too,' she went on.

'I know it is.'

'You usually go out for a walk of a Sunday. Around and about.'

'Not today. I want to finish this story.'

There was a silence, and then she said, strangely, 'That's a relief,' and left me in peace.

I did not ask myself why I needed to walk. I doubt if I had an answer, anyway. That was in my body, in its need, buried somewhere beneath intelligence.

My sister supplied the answer recently. She was talking of our father's death, and its consequences. 'Everyone cried except you. But Mother understood. "Wandering off is Peter's funny way of mourning his Dad," she said. She was right, wasn't she?'

'Yes,' I replied. 'I think she was.'

'GUTTERSNIPE'

'Your smart new friends may have bathrooms in their houses,' said my mother, during the morning inspection of ears, neck, fingernails. 'But if there's a cleaner boy in that school, I shall be very surprised.'

She reminded me that the blazer and tie I was wearing – not to mention the shirt, trousers, socks and boots –

hadn't come my way out of thin air. 'The genie didn't rub his lamp.' Now that my father had been made to retire on a small pension, money was scarce. 'You watch yourself in that playground. What gets torn has to get mended, remember.'

I was less than immaculate when I came home, with inky hands or a grazed kneecap, but I wasn't really dirty or smelly. Who, she wanted to know, was smelly? There was someone in the class, I told her, who rubbed beef dripping – that's what the rest of us thought it was – in his hair. 'He smells as if he's gone off. It's horrible when he sweats and the dripping starts to run.'

'It would be. Fine parents he must have, to let him waste good food like that. What ever can possess them? I suppose they sit down to roast beef at every meal, not once in a blue moon as we have to.'

The new games master was short and fat and pink-skinned. He was a major in the Army, and talked much of courage and pluck and discipline. When he was in charge, play was not meant to be fun.

'Have you no courage, boy?'

'Yes, sir.'

'Yes, you have, or yes, you haven't?'

'Yes, I have, sir.'

'Then show a bit of spirit. Let's see your courage in action.'

In the spring of 1949, soon after his arrival, he began to teach us how to play fives. The game dates from the seventeenth century, some years before the school was founded. The reason for its being called fives is obscure, since the scoring opens at 11 points, proceeds to 15, thence to 20, and closes at 25. It has two players, who hit a very hard ball against the four walls of a prepared court with a gloved hand.

I ducked my head when the ball came towards me, so terrified was I of its hardness.

'Use your hand, boy. The glove will protect you.'

I used my hand, and the ball dropped at my feet.

'Use your hand like a racquet, boy.'

I tried to do as he commanded, but failed at each attempt. My hand was stinging with pain, despite the protective glove.

'Shall I tell you what you are?'

'Sir?'

'You're a guttersnipe. You are a common guttersnipe.' I was aware that his pinkness had turned purple. 'Fives is for the sons of gentlemen, not guttersnipes.'

'Yes, sir.'

My mother asked me why I wasn't at school. It was only three in the afternoon.

'I've been sent home.'

'Who by?'

'The games master. He lost his temper with me. He said I was a guttersnipe.'

'He said you're what? He said you were *what?*'

'A guttersnipe.'

'I hoped I'd heard different. Are you sure he said that word?'

'Yes, I am.'

'Where's my hat and coat? I'm going round there to give him a piece of my mind.'

I pleaded with her to stay; I begged her not to embarrass me.

'Embarrass you? No one calls my son a guttersnipe and gets away with it.'

'He probably didn't mean it,' I suggested, feebly.

'If he didn't mean it, he ought not to have said it. That's his look-out.'

'Did you speak to him?'

'I did.'

She was silent.

'What did you say?'

'That's my business. Eat your tea.'

I went on asking her what she had said to my tormentor, but the question was not to be answered. I was to do my homework. The subject was closed.

*

'Your mother is a remarkable woman. Very strong-minded and forthright. You should be as proud of her as she is of you.'

'Yes, sir.'

He apologized for calling me a guttersnipe. Of course, I was no such thing. I was one of the cleanest, most well-behaved boys in the class. He wished that I was as good at sports as I was at French, English and history, but perhaps with time – and a little patience – I might improve.

(It was ventriloquial, that speech – as if he were a pink dummy on my mother's knee.)

'Thank you, sir.'

My first fives lesson was also my last. I was not required to play the sons-of-gentlemen's game again.

THE DUCHESS OF MARLBOROUGH

'Did I hear you aright or am I dreaming? You're going to play *who*?'

'The Duchess of Marlborough, Mum. Sarah, Duchess of Marlborough.'

'But she's a woman.'

'Of course she is. She was, I mean. She's been dead a long time.'

'And she's the part you've been asked to play?'

'I had to audition for it. It's the leading role. The producer found me the best.'

'Did he now? Best is as best does, and you haven't done it yet. What about the Duke?'

'What about him?'

'Well, couldn't you play him?'

'I don't want to. He doesn't have much to say. He's only a minor character. Sarah's the leading role.'

'Tell me again and I might believe you. I dread to think what your poor father would have thought, I really do. Will you be wearing clothes?'

I did not understand her question, and said so.

'Women's clothes is what I'm getting at.'

'Yes, Mum. How can I pretend to be a woman if I'm not wearing women's clothes?'

'It's no use asking me. I'm no expert, I'm sure. A son of mine a duchess! It sounds all funny to me.'

In Shakespeare's time, I said, when women were forbidden to act in public, the female characters were always played by boys. The first Juliet was a boy, and the first Ophelia, and the first Lady Macbeth.

She thanked me for the history lesson, and advised me to come down out of the clouds, because I would never be able to learn my duchess's lines if I stayed up there.

Viceroy Sarah, written by Norman Ginsbury in the 1930s as a vehicle for Edith Evans, was a virtually forgotten piece when we performed it in December 1950. Our producer, the senior English teacher, had chosen it because the school was celebrating its two-hundred-and-fiftieth anniversary, and a play that dealt with the machinations at the court of Queen Anne seemed appropriate. Our founder, being a baronet, would have had audience with her.

The course of my life was changed as a result of playing Sarah. Assuming her personality, I knew the power of artifice. For three memorable winter nights, I said goodbye to my dull self and became that creature of violent contrasts. I stormed; I screamed; I even shed real tears. I told the Queen what was good for her, and treated the wily Abigail Hill with suspicion – my involvement with Sarah was total. In costume, wig, and make-up, I was a forceful woman of the world. Acting, I understood, was a release into the nature of others. It was a wonderful way of not being Peter.

'You can keep your tantrums for the stage' became my mother's newest expression. 'Viceroy Sarah's got no place in my kitchen, putting on airs.'

She came to the opening performance. When it was over, she accepted the congratulations due to the mother of the brilliant star with a lack of surprise that disconcerted the parents of friends: 'It was no more than I expected,' she observed nonchalantly.

Before I went to bed that night, I made my customary mistake of asking for her opinion: 'What was I like?'

'You weren't like the others. They were more like themselves. They were more natural.'

I decoded this, in my need for her approval, as praise. Perhaps she was telling me, in a circuitous fashion, that I had succeeded in becoming the Duchess of Marlborough.

Perhaps.

The following December, I was the leading lady again, and rapturously happy to be free from myself.

'Emma, did you say? Emma who?'

'Emma Woodhouse.'

'Who's she when she's out?'

(This was one of my mother's favourite rhetorical questions. Only now, writing it down, am I drawn to translate it. By 'out' she meant, I think, 'out of the lunatic asylum'. Another much-used phrase was 'There are more out than in', which suggested that there were mad people walking the streets who, in her view, should have been locked up, for their own good. It followed that any woman I had been invited to play must be slightly peculiar, at least. That Emma Woodhouse, like that Viceroy Sarah, was different from the rest of us.)

She saw me as Emma, in that creaky adaptation of Jane

Austen's masterpiece, and said I came over as a 'bossy cow'.

'Thank you.'

'If I'd been that Harriet Smith, I'd have soon pulled her down a peg or two. I would have stood up for myself and told her to mind her own bloody business. I can't abide interferers.'

'Yes, Mum.'

'You just make sure you don't bring any of her behaviour back home with you.'

'You're playing *who?*'

'King Henry IV.'

'A man?'

'Of course.'

'Well, that's an improvement.'

(I had wanted to play Hotspur, but the producer insisted that the King would make greater demands on my talent. 'But he just sits on his throne and moans,' I complained. I was assured that he had reasons for moaning, which I would discover in rehearsal. I did.)

I wore a robe instead of a dress, and had a grey beard stuck to my chin with glue.

My mother said she preferred me as Sarah and Emma, for all that I was being a man at last. A person could catch the drift of what they were talking about, whereas that King went on and on and on.

47

'I can't help it,' she confessed. 'It's exactly the same with that closet music when it comes on the wireless. All those words give me a headache. That's Shakespeare's trouble, if you ask me – words.'

OUT OF WAR

My mother never forgot Matthias Hess. She forgot his name, certainly – it was foreign, and difficult to keep in your head – but the man himself, the 'true gentleman', she had no trouble remembering. 'I've stopped counting the times I've wondered what happened to that nice German prisoner,' she would say. 'I do hope his life took a turn for the better.'

His life, in the summer of 1943, could not have been worse. An artist and illustrator by profession, he was working as a farmhand in the enemy's country. He had learned, before being captured, that his wife and daughters were dead. 'They are casualties of war,' he remarked, gently. 'You, too, on your side, have such casualties.'

Instead of isolating his grief, Matthias Hess chose to unite it with the grief of thousands of others, from all the warring nations. He talked of a common sorrow. My mother often quoted him as saying that wars should only be fought by politicians and dictators, leaving the rest of the world free to go about its daily business.

'He never showed what he must have been feeling,' said my mother approvingly. 'He had every cause to, but he didn't.'

(I was too young, at six, to understand what the 'good German' was telling my mother in Uncle Bill and Aunt Phyllis's kitchen. The sound of his voice impressed me, though, and the cautious precision of his English, which he spoke with just the trace of an accent.)

The other Germans on the farm were not as friendly to their captors as Matthias Hess. They lacked his command of the enemy's language, and did not have his sanguine temperament. They concentrated on the menial work they had to do and remained aloof. One hanged himself from a tree.

We rushed to greet Matthias, my cousins and I, whenever we saw him coming along the road. Unlike most of the grown-ups we knew, he found delight in the company of children. He enjoyed hearing, as well as seeing, us, and listened with unfeigned curiosity to our breathless accounts of the day's adventures.

'Which twin are you today?' he would ask me, with mock-seriousness.

When I said I was Peter, I spoke in my own voice; when

49

I was pretending to be my twin, I adopted his gentler tones.

'But where is your brother?' The question always tested my powers of invention.

My brother, I told him, was in the castle gardens, was down in the village, was in the churchyard, was where no one could find him.

'Some twins are inseparable, but not you two. When will I see you both together?'

'Tomorrow,' I promised, and added, 'Perhaps.'

Matthias was the only adult with whom I dared to play my game of being twins, for his eyes indicated that he appreciated mischief. He affected to be as gullible as the village children, who did not know which twin was which. He allowed me to believe that I had fooled him.

'Bloody old war-monger' was how my mother described Winston Churchill. Hers was a commonly held view in south London when I was a boy. She did not alter her opinion of him after his death, as she would have done with despised neighbours or acquaintances: 'Don't speak ill of her,' she would say of a woman who hitherto had been a 'bitch' or a 'cow'. 'Now she's gone she deserves respect.' But Churchill, once gone, she continued to speak ill of. The 'war-monger' remained the 'war-monger' and did not deserve the posthumous respect she automatically afforded those she had loathed in life.

I visited her the Sunday following Churchill's state funeral and asked her if she had seen it on television.

'I watched it.'

Had she been impressed by the pomp and ceremony?

'No.'

We were silent.

'I'll tell you what I thought of while I was watching,' she said. 'I don't know why, but that nice German prisoner-of-war came into my mind, the one who did that lovely drawing of your cousin Sheila. He wanted to draw you, but you never stayed still long enough for him to get your likeness. He deserved better from life. He was what I call a true gentleman.'

MORE NATURAL

'Why can't you be more natural?' That was the question of my childhood. It was superseded by 'When are you going to marry and settle down?', the question of my twenties and early thirties. This, in turn, was replaced by 'Why don't you find yourself a proper job?', the question my mother asked in 1967, when my first book was published, and continued to ask for the next seventeen years.

How could I be more natural than natural? 'Well,' said my mother, 'you could be more like other boys.' Which other boys? 'That David, for instance.' (She didn't mean Dostoevsky David, who was less natural than I was, with his head even deeper into books.) Why should I be like him? 'Because he's natural.' In what way? 'He doesn't create.' ('Create', in my mother's vocabulary, meant 'make scenes'.) Was it natural, not to create? 'Of course. Your father never created, and nor should you.' Was it all right, then, for women to create? 'Yes.' Why was that? 'It's in their nature, that's why.'

So: had I been born a girl, I would be more natural? 'You weren't born a girl, so don't talk daft.' No, but if – *if* I were a girl – it would be natural, more natural, for me to create? 'If, if – I can't think where you get your ideas from. Yes, if you were a girl – which you're not – I'd expect you to create once in a while.' Why? 'Why? Because girls are different from boys.' It was the difference, was it, that caused girls to create? 'That's right.' And caused boys not to? 'Yes.' As simple as that? 'Yes, it's as simple as that.'

My mother believed that women were natural trouble-makers. Men had their faults, but creating wasn't one of them. God had given women feelings He hadn't seen fit to pass on to men. The world would have gone to the dogs long ago if He had.

I was told at an early age that a real man never cried. Crying was for girls and cissies. Tears were a luxury of the weak. Each time I indulged in the luxury I was mocked and cautioned: 'Who's a cry-baby, then? Who'll grow up all wrong?'

('It's a terrible thing to see a man cry,' said one of my aunts recently. She was referring to a close relative whose wife is suffering from cancer. The observation sent a chill through me, for I could hear my mother and grandmother saying it, too. Had the husband been dying instead, his wife's inevitable tears would not have been remarked upon. They would have been accounted 'natural'. What struck my aunt as terrible about the spectacle of a man in his sixties weeping was the unnaturalness of it. He was behaving, in her simple view, like a woman.)

I remember buying my mother a bunch of red roses from a florist in Chelsea. No sooner had I turned into our street than the jeering and whistling began. The proof of my suspected pansiness, I learned that day, was there in my hands, in the form of flowers.

'Why were they calling me names?' I asked my mother.

'Because it's not natural,' she replied. 'You should have got the woman in the shop to cover them up for you. It isn't natural for a boy to be seen carrying flowers.'

'Why isn't it?'

'You'll go to your grave wondering why,' she predicted accurately. 'Because it isn't, that's all.'

'But why isn't it? Please give me an answer.'

'Now, don't create. You'll know better than to carry flowers down the street again, won't you?'

It was always as simple as that. I was to accept what was natural – and more natural – and to reject what wasn't. It wasn't natural for a boy to be seen bearing flowers; it wasn't natural for a grown man to cry. How many spirits have been broken under the accumulating weight of such absurdly simple truths? The number must be beyond counting. With each childish 'Why?' I was asserting that I did not wish to be among that number.

PARIS, 1951

In the spring of 1951, I went to Paris for the first time – in my imagination. I had a story to write, and the French capital seemed the natural setting for it. I wanted my hero to run naked in the city streets, and I could not conceive that a Londoner would do anything so daring, so outlandish. He lacked the temperament.

Only the essence of the story remains with me. The details – such as my character's name: was it Jean-Paul, or was it Marcel? – have vanished. Perhaps his radio was playing Charles Trenet singing 'La Mer' (my favourite song at the time) when he got up from his desk, tore off his clothes, and ran downstairs into the busy Champs-Élysées, with its customary onion-sellers and accordion-players, who may or may not have looked askance as Jean-Paul or Marcel rushed past them in his birthday suit.

Why did he remove his shirt, his trousers, his shoes, socks and, finally, his underpants? I think I wrote that he needed to be free of his body, which was like a prison to him. Jean-Paul or Marcel was an intellectual, a man who lived in the mind. He hated his weedy physique, especially now that he was in love with a beautiful girl, who scorned and mocked him, seeing only his drab outer self, *hélas*.

His action was of the instant – spontaneous, uncalculated. He was following what he acknowledged as the dictates of his heart as he ran along the Champs-Élysées, feeling an inexplicable pride in his twenty-year-old body.

This delightful freedom, this sense of release, was brought to a swift end by an alert gendarme, who seized the naked Jean-Paul or Marcel, covered him with his cloak, and hurried him into the nearest station. The laws regarding public nudity being lenient in France (I imagined), the offender against decency was released with a warning not to repeat the offence (and some clothes, I assume).

55

Back in his apartment or hotel room, my solitary thinker took stock of his life and found it wanting. Hopelessness loomed. The pride he had felt in his paltry flesh he recognized, now, as madness, and with the recognition came fear and trembling. He picked up his manuscript from the desk and saw that the words he had written failed to convey the complexity of his thoughts. And then there was the woman, his dream-woman, and his love for her that would be for ever unrequited . . . Why continue with such an existence? Why go on?

It was in this mood of total negation that Jean-Paul or Marcel went out on to the balcony and threw himself into the teeming Paris street below.

I suppose Jean-Paul or Marcel was me, six years hence. I was skinny like him, and knew his loathing of the body. Like him, too, I had ambitions to write a work of great philosophical importance, and, like him, I was desperately in love – not with a girl, but a boy. He had a slightly Negroid look about him, and the single flaw on his otherwise perfect brown frame was the cluster of spots on his chest. They were permanent, irremovable, and I worshipped them.

When I wrote the story, I was at the beginning of a French phase. I was struck by the way French film stars dressed, by their chic raincoats, in particular. Gérard Philipe and Daniel Gélin seemed to wear raincoats in spite of, rather than because of, the weather, since it seldom rained in Paris. Three years later, when I had started earning money in my holidays from drama school, I bought my first elegant raincoat, and hoped that people would mistake me for Philipe or Gélin or Serge Reggiani, or anyone foreign.

The story was published in the school magazine, without Jean-Paul or Marcel's reckless run along the Champs-Élysées. He was fully clothed as he rushed downstairs, maddened by the arrival of spring. The editor – cutting a sentence here, re-writing another there – had craftily disposed of that essential nudity.

He did not tinker with the suicide. In Battersea, in 1951, writing about nakedness was unacceptable. Suicide, which was a crime then, was considered a fit subject for writer and reader. Had I been a French boy, I told myself, writing in a French school's magazine, Jean-Paul or Marcel would have enjoyed his brief naked excursion. They understood, over there.

KNOWING MY PLACE

'It's high time you knew your place in the world,' said my mother. 'I knew mine when I was younger than you are, with no books to help me.'

'Which place do you mean?'

'You're The Professor. You know.'

'A moment ago, you told me I didn't.'

'Didn't what?'

'Didn't know. My place in the world.'

'Well, you don't and you should is all I'm saying.'

My place, she revealed, was where I belonged, among my own kind, who weren't born to live in fancy houses or palaces but had to make do with something smaller, which didn't stop them being happy just the same.

'If God had meant you to be a duke or a lord He would have given you a duchess for a mother, not a servant like me.'

'I've no wish to be a duke. I only want to be an actor.'

'There's wanting, and then there's wanting,' she observed, mysteriously.

My mother had divided feelings about the English aristocracy, on the subject of whom she claimed to be an expert. 'They consider themselves too good for soap and water,' she said once. 'It's having handles to their names that does it, if you ask me.'

I accepted the invitation to question her further. 'Handles?'

'Yes, handles. Titles. Sirs and Ladies, Lords and such. They think it gives them the right not to wash. Some of the dirtiest objects I've ever met were lords and ladies. When you've had to scrub a gentleman's underwear, as I've had to often enough, you see a different picture from the one he likes to show the people he's supposed to be a cut above. Cut above, indeed!'

On other occasions, she spoke more charitably of the toffs who had employed her. They had their nicer side. Many of them had shown her respect, and kindness even. Our few bits of really fine china and glass (frequently dusted, but never used) had been given to her by way of thanks for her loyalty and hard work.

It was 'those others', 'those upstarts', who merited her fiercest scorn. My mother would not have understood the term *nouveau riche*, yet she was aware of the species it describes. 'They're no better than they should be. They can put on all the airs and graces, but they can't change what's inside.' Real aristocrats, she maintained, were seldom snobs, which was more than you could say for Mr and Mrs Jumped-Up, who didn't know their proper place.

*

My mother was a feudalist at heart, and subscribed to the view that the upper and lower classes had qualities in common that certain snobs and upstarts in the middle would be for ever denied. This curious view was not shared by my father, who hoped for a society in which no one was poor and everyone was equal. I inherited his hopes, refusing to believe that a malevolent God had intended me to spend my life beyond the rich man's gate.

The high time for my knowing my place never came, and furious arguments were the result of its not coming. I remember screaming at my mother that I was sick of our horrible poky kitchen, where we had to wash as well as eat, and that she shouted back that I was to know my place and not be a snob and not to think I was special, because I wasn't.

And then I said that I *was* special and would prove that I was, and then she said that she had heard little ducks fart before, and then I ran out of the house, and walked for half the night and did not return until it was nearly dawn, and found a cold rice pudding awaiting me, the familiar sign of our temporary truce.

SERVICE

Rising at dawn, with or without the lark, was the habit of my mother's lifetime. It began in 1908, when she left both school and home in order to work for the family of a Mr Fielder, the managing director of a brewery, who owned a grand house in the Hampshire village where she was born. She had just turned thirteen.

She was taken on as a menial, and it was the menials who rose earliest. They had to clear the fireplaces and start new fires; they had to lay the breakfast table; they even had to make tea for the other, superior, servants, such as the cook and the butler. My mother slept on a hard bed in one of the attics, where she froze in winter and sweltered in summer. The hours for sleep were short, she learned quickly; the remaining ones long.

She was to live thus for a further seventeen years, in the basements and attics of rich men's houses. From the Fielders she went, with a good reference, to the country seat, in that same village, of Sir Herbert Hughes-Stanton, a landscape painter and a Royal Academician. (Sir Herbert is forgotten now. Being a Fellow of the Royal Academy – being a Fellow of any Royal Society, indeed – is no insurance against artistic oblivion.) When the Hughes-Stantons moved to London, she was part of the entourage. Her first view of the city in which she was to spend the rest of her life was a pleasing one – so pleasing, in fact, that she had cause to wonder where the poor lived. It was easy to believe, as she looked down from her new attic on the broad, tree-lined street where ladies and gentlemen were strolling, that the poor did not even exist.

Her duties became more varied as she grew older. She scrubbed floors and made beds, to begin with; then she was taught how best to clean the precious furniture and silver ('with more elbow grease than polish'); then she was allowed into the kitchen, where she rolled pastry until it was fine enough for the cook to use, and then – at last – she was afforded the highest honour a maidservant could expect: 'You knew you were someone when the head butler asked you – no, *told* you – to wait at the dining table. The guests were bound to be famous.'

She was in the employment of another family, named Lyall, when she met my father. At the age of forty-one, he was working – for the first time since his return from Flanders – as a roadsweeper. He would pick her up at the tradesman's entrance to the Lyall house, and take her out for a modest evening on the town. They married in December 1925, some weeks after her thirtieth birthday.

She must have loved him deeply, for he was past having prospects. At the time of their meeting, he had only recently secured a divorce from his wife, despite the evidence of Esther's unfaithfulness in the form of a son, Cecil, who was already eight years old. My mother was aware that he had two children, the younger of whom was still in his care.

She knew she would be abandoning her humble position among the rich for a life of certain poverty.

'The lark got tired of waiting': this was my mother's greeting on those happy mornings when I lingered in bed. They were happy because my sheets were dry, and I could rise without feeling abject or humiliated.

'Some of us,' she said, referring to herself, 'have been up and about since six.'

She always made the remark proudly. In her view, rising early meant that you were ready and willing to meet the day's challenges; that you acknowledged there was work to be done, and the sooner the better. 'The hours you waste in there,' she said, pulling the bedclothes off me, 'will never come round again.'

'Loving your work represents the best, most concrete approximation of happiness on earth,' observes Libertino Faussone, the hero of Primo Levi's novel *The Wrench*. This was Levi's own judgement, too, and my mother would have echoed it. 'Work is all I understand and all I've ever understood,' she declared in 1980, when she made the reluctant decision to take a permanent rest. 'I shall go mad,' she threatened, 'with nothing to do. I shall lose my wits, just sitting about.'

Her restless nature would not permit her to just sit about. She found work to do, where there was none – dusting a spotlessly clean ornament, perhaps, or polishing a surface she had polished earlier that morning. It was impossible for her to stop what she had been doing for seventy-two years – the length of her working life. Confined, now, to the small flat she shared with my sister, she often railed against the infirmities of an old age that was denying her the pleasure of 'providing a service'. She telephoned me one afternoon after her retirement and, when I asked her how she was, she started to cry: 'I'm so bored,' she managed to say. 'I never thought I'd be bored like this.'

My father had started to work for the council just before he married my mother. His roadsweeper's wages were meagre, and had to be accounted for to the last farthing. It wasn't long before my mother resumed her work as a domestic – but as a cleaner now. Her equally meagre wages at least ensured that their two children – the son, born in 1927; the daughter, in 1931 – could be fed and clothed. When I was conceived, to my parents' surprise, the need for money became even more urgent. During the war, my mother went to work, as a vegetable cook, at Buckingham Palace. 'The staff were given a bonus every Christmas,' she told me in the final year of her life. 'A crisp ten-shilling note in an embossed envelope. We all had to wait in line to receive it from His Majesty. When it came to my turn, I curtsied, as was proper, and then he gave me my envelope. He had a white glove on the hand he used for shaking the hands of his servants.'

Her references, she boasted, were always glowing. The glamorous divorcée in Chelsea, who looked like the Duchess of Windsor, passed my mother on to a lord and lady of her acquaintance who, in turn, recommended her to Prince Georg and Princess Anne of Denmark, her last employers. She adored the Princess, whom she awarded her greatest accolade: 'The nice thing about Princess Anne is that she's *natural*.'

One Sunday, a week or so after her retirement, my mother received an invitation to have lunch with the Princess at her cottage in Hertfordshire. She was driven there by the Prince's chauffeur in a limousine in which she felt lost.

'It was a lovely day,' she reported. 'The Princess cooked the meal herself, and we had wine and coffee and petits fours. You wouldn't have thought you were with royalty, it was that natural.'

There was, however, one blemish on this otherwise perfect occasion. 'She wouldn't let me wash the dishes. It really upset me. I insisted, but she wouldn't have it. "I'll do the washing-up when you've gone," she said. She couldn't understand me when I told her that it was all wrong. It was my place to do the washing-up, not hers. I didn't have the nerve to say that I would do it better, having had to do it all my born days.'

I remarked that the Princess was being kind and considerate to someone she respected.

'That's all very well,' my mother answered. 'But I still

maintain the Princess was in the wrong. I wanted to show her my gratitude, in the only way I know.'

CAPEESH?

I loved to hear my father say 'I fancy jellied eels for my supper tonight' because the familiar words always ensured ice-cream and mystery for me. 'Take the jug to Maggy Brown's, son, and have the man fill it right up to the top.'

Maggy Brown's pie and eel shop (known to everyone as the 'pieneel') was usually crowded on Friday evenings. I could not understand why so many people wanted to eat eels. I had watched an uncle kill them with a hammer and had seen them go on wriggling after they were supposed to be dead. I had heard that snakes did the same. From that horrifying day onward, snakes and eels became indistinguishable in my imagination. 'Do they taste of snake?' I had asked my uncle. 'Not having ever eaten a snake,' he'd replied, 'I wouldn't know. But snakes don't swim, and eels do.'

(His explanation did not satisfy me. Eels, I decided, were watery snakes.)

As soon as the jug was filled – not *quite* to the top – and I had covered it with a cloth ('to keep the germs out'), I hurried home to collect my reward. With the threepenny-bit my father gave me for acting as his errand-boy, I could treat myself to a vanilla or strawberry or chocolate ice-cream from the Italian ice-cream parlour in the High Street.

(My mother was not alone in calling its owners Nea*lo*pitans. For some reason, still obscure to me forty years later, 'Neopolitan' was one of those words that got adjusted when spoken, along with 'bronchial' which was transformed into 'bronichal', and 'mischievous', which was always 'mischevious'.)

Listening to the Neapolitans, I knew delight of a strange kind. It hardly mattered that I did not understand what they were saying to one another: the sound of their voices was enchantment enough. The oldest Neapolitans, husband and wife, both dressed in black, did most of the talking. They sat on either side of a table at the rear of the shop and issued a stream of commands (I imagined) to their son and daughter-in-law behind the counter. Almost every sentence seemed to end on a rising inflection with a word I transcribed in my mind as *capeesh. Capeesh?* they would wonder, or enquire, or – more often – demand, and they would be answered in Italian, or with a nod, or in exasperated Cockney English, which bewildered, and temporarily silenced, them.

I was happiest when all three generations of the Neapolitan family were in the shop, for those were times of much *capeesh*-ing. I envied the children their gift of being able to switch in an instant from colloquial English to the mysterious language of their parents and grandparents. With the switch came a change in their bodies as well as their voices: I was aware, as they responded to the inevitable *capeesh?*, of hands suddenly coming to life. I could sense, even then, that these were articulate hands, as necessary to complete communication as the words they were accompanying. Returning to south London from Southern Italy, they let their hands become mere hands again – anonymous, ineloquent.

I licked my ice-cream slowly, and stayed as long as possible in the parlour where I memorized my first Italian word, not knowing then that *capisc'?* means 'understand?'.

Eighteen years later, on a balmy May evening, I wandered into the Gardens of the Royal Palace in Naples, after enjoying a simple meal of *spaghetti al pomodoro*, cheese, fruit and wine in a *trattoria* on Via Roma. I was alone in the city, awaiting the arrival of a Florentine friend, with whom I was to set off on a tour of Calabria.

I sat down on a bench, where I was joined shortly by an uncharacteristically shy Neapolitan, who smiled at me nervously before averting his face from my admiring gaze.

'Mi scusa,' I began, and told him, in what I considered to be my best Italian, how much I loved Naples, which for me was even more beautiful than Rome. He was silent. I gabbled on, about Capri now, and the lovely day I'd had there, and how I'd visited the *Grotta azzurra* with a newly-married couple from Bologna, and how the three of us had taken lunch at a restaurant on the island. He was still silent.

Was it my accent? Was I using the wrong words? 'Lei capisce?' I asked, in desperation.

'I am very sorry,' he said, haltingly, 'but I am Swedish. You speak, perhaps, English?'

'I am English,' I said, and then we both laughed, and then the improbably dark-haired, but blue-eyed, Swede and I went off together.

I remembered the Battersea Neapolitans and their *capeesh-ing* when I was staying, in the winter of 1983, in a small town in the far north of Scotland. A friend had a house there, which she lived in during the summer. She had heard that I needed a quiet place to write in, and had offered me this quietest of places for an entire month. All I could hear sometimes was the weather.

On my first afternoon, I discovered a curious sweetshop-cum-café in the town's one really lively street. It had a Christmas display in the window, and every single item was Italian – boxes of chocolates from Perugia, *panforte* from Siena, bottles of Amaro and Campari. I went inside, and was greeted by a friendly Scottish woman standing behind an espresso machine. She remarked that she had never seen me before, and I explained that I was here for a short holiday. She looked startled. 'A holiday? Here? In late November?' It was a *working* holiday, I said. I had a lot of studying to do, in peace and quiet. She grinned. 'There's plenty of peace and quiet here, and some to spare.'

She brought me a coffee and a slice of *panforte*, and unravelled the simple mystery of the Italian display. She had met her husband, a Neapolitan, during the war. He had been taken prisoner, and sent to work on a farm in the countryside near Inverness. They had fallen in love, and he had remained in Scotland, where they had opened this little business and raised a family. She had had to learn Italian, because he was hopeless at languages. He'd only ever heard Scots, which still perplexed him, forty years on.

Capisc'? There it was, my magic word, coming from a back room. The sound of it made me smile. It was a man speaking, and he was answered, in Italian, by two young women, who presently appeared, greeting their mother in Scottish English. They had thick black hair and brown eyes. Seeing them, I was reminded of those Friday evenings when my father's passion for jellied eels had to be satisfied, and I was his eager errand-boy.

I returned to the unlikely café several times, and occasionally ate a *granita di limone* – a real Italian water-ice, delicate and sharp, and not at all like the cloying and sickening stodge I was happy to eat as a boy.

THE NEW FACE

Sam and Mary were friends of my parents who lived in a grand house near Clapham Common. They looked after me during what my mother referred to as 'difficult times' – the long school holidays. Although they were elderly, they never lost patience with the inquisitive boy who had been entrusted to them. They answered most of my questions, and even let me join in some of their conversations. These were rare privileges.

Sam was a survivor of Flanders, and so was his brother, who had – to my childish ears – the strangest name in the world. I pictured it written down as *Eef*. 'Call me Uncle Eef,' he'd instructed me on our first meeting.

('Why's he called Eef, Mum?'

'Because that's what his mother and father chose for him.'

'It sounds funny.'

'I dare say it does.')

'We're both out of the Bible, my brother and I,' Sam explained. 'I'm Samuel, and Eef's Ephraim. I'm the more important because I've got two books named after me. Eef only warrants a bit of a chapter in Genesis.'

Sam and Mary's house was no grander, no larger, than the hundreds of other houses built in Clapham in the second half of the nineteenth century. It seemed vast to me, because I was always coming to it from the constriction – the sometimes suffocating constriction – of our tiny back-street home.

It is Mary's kitchen, in particular, that looms largest in memory. ('You could swing a lion in there, let alone a cat,' my father had once remarked.) Mary was Scottish, and proud of her country's cuisine, which she delighted in cooking. She made her own scones and her own marmalade. A bowl of lumpless porridge was set before me as soon as I arrived in the morning, whatever the season. 'To make you brawny,' she said. 'There's nothing of you yet.'

I would sit at the long, wide kitchen table, eating the tripe and cow-heel Mary had prepared for lunch, and listen to Sam and Eph and Alec as they discussed the state of post-war Britain. Alec was a Scot, too. He stayed in the house when the people he worked for were 'travelling abroad' or 'having a quiet evening to themselves'. Alec smiled at me when he imparted this curious information.

'You'll be off to Scotland soon, won't you, Alec?'

'Ay, that I will. They're having their bags packed at this moment, if I'm not mistaken.'

Who were these people, who had their bags packed for them?

'You wouldn't believe me if I told you,' Alec replied. 'They have a big house in London, and another in Norfolk, and another in Scotland, which is where I'll be joining them in a week or so.'

'Are they bigger houses than this one, Alec?'

'Miles bigger. Miles and miles and miles bigger.'

'Like palaces?'

I waited, mystified, until their laughter subsided.

'Yes, Peter, you could say they're like palaces. A little like palaces, yes.'

And then they laughed again.

'Ach, Alec, stop teasing the lad,' said Mary.

That house was palace enough for me. I went there – by trolleybus, by tram, or on foot – in anticipation of pleasure. There was the pleasure of Mary's food; of Sam's amiable company; of Alec, dressed in kilt and sporran and with a dagger in his sock, educating me in the customs of his country. There was the pleasure, too, of space, and of being at liberty in it, for Sam and Mary allowed me to wander where I fancied. Of all their many rooms, the bathroom was the most magical. I was unused to running hot water, and loved turning on the tap and washing my hands and face a dozen or more times a day. I could be really immaculate here, I thought, with none of the embarrassing palaver I had to undergo at our kitchen sink. I was happiest when I stayed overnight, because that meant getting into, and lingering in, the bath itself. There was no attendant to tell me my ten minutes were up, though Sam occasionally wondered if I'd gone to sleep and drowned.

In the years immediately following my father's death, I was a constant guest at Sam and Mary's house. They often took a nap after lunch, and it was then that I read the book I had borrowed from the library on Lavender Hill. There were any number of rooms to read in, but I usually chose the conservatory, in which Sam had been busy all morning with his beloved plants. My serious reading began in Clapham, for Sam and Mary, seeing me in 'another world', would leave me in it, secure in the knowledge that I was in the only place I wanted to be.

I could listen to music there, and not be interrupted. Neither Sam nor Mary shared my taste for the classics, but – as Mary observed – 'The door is thick, and if you keep it closed we shan't hear the noise.' They had a real gramophone that didn't require winding up every five minutes. I played my few precious records on it – Sibelius's *Finlandia*, Tchaikovsky's 'Fantasy' overture to *Romeo and Juliet*, and Ravel's *Pavane for a Dead Infanta*, which was conducted by Guido Cantelli, who was soon to become my absolute hero.

'Why does my pen not drop from my hand on approaching the infinite pity and tragedy of all the past?' Henry James asks himself in his *Notebooks*. My own pencil has now to record something – by which I mean a mere particle, a jot – of the pity and tragedy Sam, Mary and their only son,

Roy, endured throughout and beyond the years I knew them.

Roy trained in the Air Force, and became a fighter pilot soon after the outbreak of war. One night in 1942, he set off on a mission with a co-pilot and a navigator. The plane came under German attack and was shot down in flames. Roy alone survived, his face and body horribly burned.

Sam and Mary often talked of Roy to me, always with pride. There were photographs of him on the mantelpiece in the sitting-room – as a boy, and as a handsome young man in uniform. They did not prepare me, those loving snapshots, for the Roy I met in the house one summer's day when the war was over. I had not seen a face like his, ever – with eyes that seemed to be stitched into his skin, which was red and raw and looked as if it might explode.

I stared at him, out of curiosity as much as horror. He had a smile in his voice that his face couldn't manage when he greeted me. 'Hello, Peter. I've heard a lot about you.'

Sam and Mary were confident, then, that Roy would be happy. The nurse who had tended him in the hospital at Roehampton had become his wife and borne him a daughter, with whom I played when she was six or seven. (I remember telling her a story that I invented on the spot, and – later – frightening her by turning up the volume on her grandparents' radio during a performance of the 'Eroica'. She screamed and screamed.) That summer, Roy had a family, and a job, and a house in the suburbs, and the expectation of a pleasant life ahead.

When I last saw Sam and Mary, they were living in a small flat, not far from their old house. Mary was frail, and confined to bed. She was in her nineties, and her mind was wandering, but she recognized my mother and me before drifting back to sleep. Sam, at ninety-six, was almost as sprightly and upright as he had been when I was a boy. He had a dog who demanded a great deal of exercise, which Sam made certain that he got. 'I still walk five miles every day,' Sam boasted. 'I have to, to keep that so-and-so quiet.'

Sam served us tea and biscuits – not Mary's, for she was past cooking now. My mother wondered how Roy was doing, and Sam replied that his second marriage appeared to be working out all right. As for business, you couldn't go wrong with a pub. Roy, we learned, was a publican in a very well-to-do town in the country.

And I learned, that day, that Ephraim was dead ('He didn't have his older brother's hold on life,' Sam said affectionately); that Alec had been employed at Buckingham Palace ('He piped the King and Queen in to dinner'), and that Mary had worked there, too, as a vegetable cook, which job she had passed on to my mother, when Roy was shot down. 'Did you really work at the palace?' I asked my mother. 'Yes,' she answered. 'Why didn't you tell me?' 'Because I didn't want the whole of Battersea to know.'

At the door, as we were leaving, Sam said, 'I've only one hope left, and that's that Mary goes before I do. You've seen how she is. I wouldn't like to have her nursed by strangers.'

Mary died, and so, soon afterwards, did her contented husband, suddenly, with little pain.

I was reading the newspaper one morning, idly, flicking from page to page, when I came across an item that seemed familiar. It had to do with the suicide of a fighter pilot who had, according to the coroner who was giving his verdict on the unhappy case, 'served his country bravely'. It was then that I saw Roy's name. The coroner informed the court that Roy had a 'long history of depression', brought on by the terrible incident in which he had been involved. His first marriage had failed as a result of this depression, and the fact that Roy had started to drink heavily. These fits of uncontrollable misery had continued into his second marriage, and so had the heavy drinking. He had killed himself in the middle of the night, leaving a note that stated simply that he could not go on. The coroner then expressed sorrow, and gave his verdict of suicide, 'while the balance of the deceased's mind was disturbed'.

We talk of the courage of the infirm and maimed, seldom of the despair they must, inevitably, endure. Roy was extraordinarily courageous, not least in the manner of his dying. He had waited until his parents were dead before succumbing to the full weight of his distress.

I think of Sam and Mary brightening the childhood of someone else's son, while their own son lay in a London hospital, his face and body for ever transfigured; and I think of Roy, seeing that strange new face whenever he looked in a mirror – a face that must have reminded him of a certain night, when his two friends were consumed in the flames, and he was dragged free, to go on living, as best he could.

THE WIRELESS

'It's worse than a cat being strangled' was my mother's stock response to the sound of the music I wanted to hear. 'Put the poor creature out of her misery' meant that she wanted me to turn off the wireless when Elisabeth Schwarz-kopf or Sena Jurinac, or any other of those 'squawking foreign cows', was singing. 'I've got nerves, if she hasn't. She must be giving herself a terrible headache.'

The wireless rested on top of an old chest-of-drawers

in the kitchen. It didn't come to automatic life when you turned the switch, as our neighbours' radios did. It had to be coaxed, cajoled, and thumped. My mother knew exactly how to thump it, for it always responded to her fist. 'You don't have the touch,' she would remark on those frustrating occasions when my hand hit the set in vain. 'You haven't learnt the knack. I'm glad there's one thing in the world I know that you don't.'

This knowledge, this secret skill, gave her a power over the wireless she could exercise at whim. Fierce rows broke out when she refused to apply the required thump, because she had no intention of listening to what she described as 'closet music'. I remember one unhappy evening when a performance of Brahms's *St Anthony Chorale Variations* came and went, splutteringly. I begged her to adjust the set. She continued ironing, and did not bother to conceal the pleasure she was taking in my annoyance.

In the days immediately after the death of King George VI, in 1952, the wireless played solemn music round the clock. My mother's thumps brought forth Bach, Mozart, Beethoven, Handel. 'Oh, my God, not more of it. Closet, closet, closet, all day long. It'll drive me mad, if it hasn't already.'

During that wonderful week or so, my musical education was broadened considerably. I heard several masterpieces for the first time: Wagner's *Siegfried Idyll*, Schubert's

C Major Symphony. I sat at the kitchen table, entranced.

'I wish kings died more often,' I said to my mother when the solemn tribute was over.

Although she was clearly relieved, she snapped back that I was not to be so wicked, I was to show respect for the dead, especially if they were royal.

There was one musician who was spared comparison with the strangled cat or the operatic cow. Kathleen Ferrier, my mother decided, was 'natural'. 'She doesn't squawk, like those foreign cows do.' We didn't bicker while Ferrier was singing, and the wireless was afforded its necessary thump if the sound suddenly vanished. Her recording of 'Che farò' or 'What is Life?', as it was anglicized, from Gluck's *Orfeo* moved my mother almost to tears. How much this feeling was inspired by Ferrier's early death I can't say, but I recall the delight I felt in my mother's attentiveness towards a great artist performing great music. I still find it odd that Gluck, of all composers, was the only one who ever enchanted her, albeit with a single aria.

My mother and I often listened to the Sunday night serial together. She couldn't read Dickens or Jane Austen or Robert Louis Stevenson – 'I'm not a lady of leisure, and I don't have the brain for all those words' – yet she enjoyed the adaptations of their novels on the wireless. She once observed, shrewdly, that the adaptors had 'cut out the boring and difficult bits' – the near-truth of which observation I would shortly discover. She was as frightened as I was by the six episodes of Conan Doyle's *The Lost World*, in which Professor Challenger and his fellow explorers confronted dinosaurs and pterodactyls somewhere in Southern America.

We were either united or divided by our constantly thumped wireless. Unity or division was determined by what was coming out of the 'cantankerous bloody thing'. 'I regret the day you first heard that closet music. It's made you moonier and moodier, if you ask me.'

Had it not been for the wireless, which was never called the radio, I would have lived without the 'strangled cat' and the 'foreign cow', besides much else that was instructive and entertaining.

'There's a concert on tonight, Mum.'

'Is there really?'

'Can I listen to it?'

She does not commit herself.

'Some of it?'

She remains silent.

'Please, Mum.'

'Will there be squawking?'

'No, it's a symphony.'

'Well, we'll just have to see what frame of mind the wireless is in, won't we?'

OTHER PEOPLE'S RELICS

'That's come all the way from India,' said my mother, pointing to a small brass-topped table. Visitors were impressed by this relic of the Raj, which had a double function – the brass top could do service as a tray, being detachable, and the three legs could be folded into one another to make a single leg ('just like a concertina') when they weren't needed.

'Funny to think it's ended up in our front room after the places it's been. The people who passed it on to me ate what they called their tiffin off it.'

These people, these passers-on of now unwanted relics, were my mother's various employers. Most of our possessions had once been theirs. The black wooden elephants with the missing tusks ('made of real ivory') that faced each other from either end of the mantelpiece had lost them in grander surroundings – in some huge nursery, I liked to imagine, where the rich man's carefree children were no respecters of real ivory. Between the elephants were three monkeys who heard, spoke and saw no evil: you could tell which was which by the hands that covered ears, mouth and eyes. My mother, who pretended not to relish gossip, advised me to follow their example. 'If you do as the monkeys do, you won't come to much harm.'

'But you don't do as they do.'

'And what do you mean by that?'

'You don't speak well of the gypsies.'

'I'd soon speak well of them if they changed their habits. Until they do, I shall speak as I find.'

From some other family's nursery (the Fielder children's? the Hughes-Stantons'?) came a beautifully carved chest-of-drawers. It measured twelve inches in height and nineteen in width. The drawers were framed on either side by an Ionic column.

Was it made for a dwarf, I wondered?

'Don't be wicked. No, it wasn't. It's out of a doll's house. The mummy doll had it in the best bedroom, to keep her fresh clothes in.'

'The best bedroom? Weren't the other bedrooms as good then?'

A proper doll's house, my mother explained, was a copy of a gentleman's house, only smaller; which meant that it had a best, or master, bedroom, as well as bedrooms for the children and bedrooms for the servants, up in the attics. It would also have a drawing-room (people who were no better than they should be called it a lounge) and a study or library, and a nursery, and a kitchen with pantry – had that answered my question?

'Was there any other furniture?'

'Of course there was. Chairs, tables, sideboards – even a grand piano, if my memory serves me right.'

Where were the chairs and tables now, and why hadn't we got them?

'They're scattered here and there, I suppose. Things vanish while you're busy blinking. That little chest-of-drawers was all that was left. We're lucky to have it.'

'I've never known a boy so ungrateful,' snapped my mother when I complained about the wind-up gramophone that had been passed on to her to pass on to me. 'You can't expect the latest model when you're paying nothing.'

It was the effort I had to put into making it work that maddened me: turning and turning and turning the handle for a mere four or five minutes of sound, and not very lovely sound at that. It simply wasn't worth the strain.

'You're lucky to have it at all. It was given to me to give to you, because I told them how fond you are of closet music. They had to hunt high and low to find it.'

'Why?'

'Well, because they'd stopped using it, I suppose. But it's in good condition, and there's a tin full of new needles.'

My frantic winding guaranteed that Charles Trenet sang

most of 'La Mer' and 'Clopin Clopant' in a moderate approximation of his real voice, before being overcome with lethargy at the close of the record. It was when an entire orchestra was afflicted by this sluggishness that I grew incensed. Short as it is, Tchaikovsky's *Romeo and Juliet* overture – on both sides of four 78s – still made excessive demands on my right hand, which I had to keep employed to prevent the violins becoming tired cellos, the cellos double-basses. Only once did I hear the overture from start to finish, as Tchaikovsky might have intended it to be heard, but the memory of the stress involved in averting orchestral languor ensured that I didn't try playing it again.

There was no need to, anyway, for Sam and Mary had an up-to-date radiogram, run by electricity. I could listen to my records now without anxiety or frustration.

The passed-on wind-up gramophone was passed on to a neighbour, who was – my mother assured me – 'more grateful for it than a certain person I could mention'.

Whatever was passed on to us, we were lucky to have. My mother accepted everything she was offered, on the principle that, if you turned something down that you didn't like the look of, you might not be given the opportunity to take something you did. We were lucky to have the ugly objects because they were old-fashioned and therefore valuable – 'Not that I would ever dream of selling them' – while the ones she considered pretty gave our front room a touch of class not to be found in the other front rooms in the street. Those passed-on glasses and remnants of tea or dinner services had flaws that weren't immediately visible to admiring guests, who weren't invited to examine them closely. A pair of fluted art nouveau bowls graced the top of the passed-on sideboard. My mother kept them filled with apples and oranges, for an aesthetic as much as a practical reason – the brownness of the glass ('it's got something in it, I don't know what, that makes it unbreakable') needed brightening up a bit with a splash of colour, and fresh fruit did the trick to perfection.

Books, or 'dust traps', were not regarded with the admiration deemed fit for china or furniture, perhaps because the neighbours – who, like my mother, referred to weekly or monthly magazines as 'books' – distrusted them as time-wasters. Bound books, with the exception of the obligatory Bible and certain popular encyclopaedias and manuals of home medicine, were absent from most of the houses in the street.

My mother thought new books looked better in a room than old ones, which – as she observed of the copy of *Nicholas Nickleby* my father brought home for me – 'gave off a nasty smell'. A souvenir volume, published to celebrate the coronation of George VI and Queen Elizabeth, was the one she exhorted her children to value most – its subject being royalty, it was worthier of respect than the passed-on novels of G. A. Henty, or *Alice* with its Tenniel drawings, or Fitzgerald's translation of *The Rubáiyát* of Omar Khayyám, decorated by Edmund Dulac.

*

'Passed on' was, and is, a euphemism for 'dead'. My mother used the phrase in preference to 'handed down' when she talked of the stuff she had been given over many years. 'Handed down' smacked too much of the charity she despised. 'I've never taken charity, and I never will' – and of a particular kind of poverty. It was all right to hand things down – clothes, mostly – within the family, but not outside it. Everything else was passed on.

When my mother and sister were informed that the house was due to be demolished and that they were to be moved to a brand new council flat, they agreed to make a 'clean sweep'. A new flat called for new furnishings, new ornaments. The hoarded and treasured were suddenly the abandoned, and 'old-fashioned' became a pejorative, rather than a respectful, term. My mother looked at the cracked antique plates and the chipped glasses with a fresh eye, and saw their flaws more clearly. They were disposed of, along with the best dining table and the chest-of-drawers from the big doll's house, as things belonging to a vanished age. Other people, myself included, now possess those relics.

TOBY JUGS

I had two close schoolfriends named David – one exception-
ally clever, the other of only ordinary intelligence. It was
the second David my mother liked. She found him 'natural'.
He was not burdened, as the first David and her younger
son were, with brains.

(At the age of thirteen, the first David was working his
way through the novels of Dostoevsky. I remember his
being amused by the name of the pawnbroker in *The House
of the Dead*: Isay Bumshtein. The forbidding intellectual
could still giggle at the naughty word 'bum'.)

The second David was the calmest person I have ever
known. He had red hair, but there was no fire in his nature.
He was considered dull by the livelier boys in the class,
because of a quality of indifference in him – a quality
gained, perhaps, from his unwanted knowledge of Kipling's
'If', the one poem his father knew by heart and was fond
of quoting, in a voice put on for the purpose.

It was his very calmness that drew me to David, for I
was frantically ambitious then, convinced that I would be
a great classical actor by my mid-twenties. He believed me
when I said that I was going to play Hamlet at the Old Vic.
He was pleased to know someone who had his whole future
planned, since he had no plans at all. He invited me to

gabble on about myself – and gabble I did, while he listened, in his calm way, thinking I don't know what.

David's father was a taxi-driver, but not by choice. He had had a distinguished career in the Army, he assured me when I first met him. 'Fell on bad times,' he explained. 'That's why I'm driving a bloody taxi.'

He wore a blazer and a bow-tie, this gentleman-cabbie, and cavalry-twill trousers and suede shoes. He smoked Turkish cigarettes. When his wife wasn't present, he talked to David and me as a 'man of the world', hinting at numerous exotic women he had enjoyed on his trips abroad.

David's father's face was uniformly purple, his nose of an even purpler shade. Why was it that strange colour? 'Drink,' answered David, stating a matter of fact. 'Whisky. My father's a drunkard.'

'My father's a drunkard': David's mother would have been appalled if she had known he had been so honest. It was one of the major tasks of her marriage to pretend that her husband was the best man any woman could want. She looked at him with a pride that occasionally verged on the fearful, as if she anticipated his saying or doing something embarrassing, despite the presence in the room of David's friend. 'Oh, no,' I heard her say once, in her wariness. 'No, no, please don't.' A minute later, heeding her caution, he slammed himself out of their perpetually untidy mews house.

I liked her for her untidiness, and also because she was young and pretty. David's life at home was wonderfully relaxed and carefree, I thought, compared to mine. When the three of us played Monopoly, I would be desolate if I didn't manage to secure a fortune, but David's indifference to success and failure alike usually manifested itself in the form of a shrug. 'If' was printed on a scroll that hung on the wall above the expensive radiogram the drunken husband and father had bought them – as the result of a successful flutter, probably. One, at least, of its varied recipes for manhood had been tried and tested.

Besides 'If', besides the comfortable furniture covered with the hairs of the family's two Sealyhams, there were hundreds – it seemed – of toby jugs. David's mother collected them, and during the years of our friendship the collection expanded alarmingly. There they were, those complacent fat squires, with their cheeks ruddy from beer, in their three-cornered hats, smoking their pipes – looking down from the shelves that had been specially built for them on the doting collector for whom drink did not often signify cheeriness or good fellowship. She was safe among her china guzzlers, which she washed and dusted regularly.

I was not aware then, as I think I am now, that David's calmness had been acquired in a school of pain I was spared attending. The former officer and gentleman who preferred to pick up his fares in Belgravia, Kensington and Chelsea had taught him much that a child ought not to know about deceit and weakness. David's calm and benevolent character was his willed gift to his friends, of whom – for a happy time – I was privileged to be the closest.

I see him, as I have seen him in dreams, surrounded by those rubicund china faces, those Victorian visions of a feudal England, which so appeased his unhappy mother. I last heard from him when I was in my twenties and not playing Hamlet at the Old Vic. He wrote to say that he had married.

PANSY AND OSCAR WILDE

'The theatre is a breeding-ground for pansies,' a concerned relation warned me. 'And they say most actresses are prostitutes.'

'Do they?'

'It's common knowledge.'

'Is it?'

'Of course it is. You ought to know that. You're supposed to be the brainy one in the family.'

I received many such warnings in the months before I began training for the stage at the Central School of Speech and Drama. Pansy-boys and prostitutes were the kind of people I would be mixing with, come September. There was still time for me to see reason and change my mind.

This reasonable, and occasionally expert, advice ('I've made a study of theatricals,' claimed an uncle, 'and they're all tarred with the same filthy brush') was given to me, gratis, by whoever visited our house. Nothing was said about the insecurity of the average actor's life, for of that scrap of common knowledge my relatives and neighbours seemed unaware. It was only the sin they knew, and worried, about – those mucky goings-on that actors and actresses got up to as soon as the show was over.

'They'll have you in their cesspit, if you don't watch out.'

I did not, could not, reveal to them that I was what they called a 'pansy'. They would not have believed me, anyway. I came from working stock, and my ancestors had toiled long and hard to make a humble living. It was common knowledge that pansies were the sons of the idle rich, who had nothing better to do than be waited on, hand and foot. Pansies had weak blood – blood as weak as water – in their veins. You wouldn't find a pansy in our part of London.

Across the river, yes, in Kensington – where, it was pointed out to me, the Central School was situated – but not here, not in Battersea.

I was a Battersea pansy, wary of displaying his true colours in the sunlight. I belonged, as did so many others of the same peculiar genus, in the shade. That was where we had to function, if at all, in the days when we were accounted criminals.

Why 'pansy'? The flower is a hardy biennial, as easy to grow as it is adaptable. It was developed from the native *Viola tricolor* by the gardener, Mr T. Thompson, in 1810, but a mere twenty-five years later there were 400 different kinds of pansy in existence, in a wide range of colours. Perhaps it is this more flamboyant bloom ('Sutton's Giant Fancy', 'Englemann's Giant', 'Winter Sun' and 'Perfection Mixed' are among the most popular varieties) rather than the traditional viola known as 'heartsease' and 'love-in-idleness' that inspired some wit in the nineteenth century to compare it with the male homosexual. The innocent Mr Thompson, straining for ever-bolder combinations of colours, may be unknowingly responsible for the word's secondary definition.

'Pansy' was the word my family used whenever the 'love that dare not speak its name' was spoken of, derisively. Oscar Wilde was mentioned, too: 'He looks like an Oscar Wilde to me'; 'He's the Oscar Wilde type'; 'I know an

Oscar Wilde when I see one'. These Oscar Wilde's were invariably famous, with their photographs in the papers – actors, principally; ballet dancers, painters, composers.

People in our street, ignorant of his plays, essays and poems, had heard about the strange flower Wilde wore in his buttonhole. There was a joke. 'Be careful where you bend over,' it went, 'or you might find that Oscar Wilde behind you, sticking his green carnation in a place he shouldn't.'

Such was the nature of Wilde's fame in south London fifty years after his death. I had knowledge of him – common knowledge – long before I read, and admired, his works: as a menace to small boys; as a scented so-and-so who deserved to go to prison, where he ought to have been strung up; as 'one of them' or 'one of those'; as – how often it was said – 'a big fat pansy'.

AT THE DANISH COURT
(with Romeo, Bleeding Macbeth and Hamlet's Sister)

Two things were certain: I was going to play Hamlet and I was going to die young. The second of these eventualities I would leave to chance, but the first required preparation.

In the summer of 1952, at various times of the day and night, I studied with a thoroughness that still astonishes me. I learned every line of *Hamlet* by heart.

People have done madder things, I assured myself as I committed the words of Reynaldo, the Sailor, the Players and Rosencrantz and Guildenstern to memory. Learning *Hamlet* was no more idiotic than climbing a mountain or swimming the English Channel. The play was *there*, after all, as huge and challenging, in its way, as any Everest. The difference was that I would be conquering it in an upstairs room, in a terraced house in Battersea, in secret.

I spent weeks and weeks in and out of Elsinore, a self-invited guest at the Danish court. 'I'm not going to tell you again that your supper's on the table,' announced my mother, banging on the door. 'I don't know what the street must think,' she remarked when I emerged, book in hand. 'All that spouting every evening.'

'Let them think what they want,' I answered. 'They're welcome to their thoughts.'

'You're making us a laughing stock with your eternal bloody Shakespeare.'

To Emily, who lived on the ground floor with her husband and two daughters, Shakespeare was Shakespoke. 'Your boy lives for his Shakespoke,' she said to my mother. 'Yes, and I wish he didn't,' was the response.

'There goes Bleeding Macbeth,' Emily would say whenever I began to spout. Why she chose Macbeth, and why she had him bleeding, I never discovered. 'Oh, my God, it's Bleeding Macbeth having one of his turns,' I heard her call up the stairs once. 'Give the poor sod a dagger and tell him where to stick it.'

I was indifferent to such taunts, as I was to those of the neighbourhood children. 'Romeo, Romeo, wherefore are you, Romeo,' they shouted after me. I walked on, muttering lines that weren't Romeo's. 'What've you gone and done with Juliet? Put a bun in her oven, have you, you dirty tosser?'

With Gertrude in mind, I asked my mother if she ever considered marrying another man. 'Don't be so wicked,' she snapped.

'What's wicked about it?'

It was wicked because it insulted my father's memory. 'I won't find his like twice in a lifetime,' she said. 'However hard I look – which I shan't be doing, while there's breath in my body.'

I think it was Michael's idea to write a play with Hamlet's sister as the principal character. Michael was one of my close friends. My mother approved of him because he had once congratulated her on the way she made tea, which was more than her son ever had. We enjoyed acting together: he was Queen Anne to my Duchess of Marlborough, and Mrs Elton in what the adaptor had left of *Emma*.

We called our verse drama *Hamela*. We wrote three or four scenes before the effort of finding rhymes caused us to admit defeat. Our Hamela was a lively, commonsensical girl, who regarded Hamlet as an absolute drip. It was her opinion that their father's death was really nothing to brood over. On the battlements at dawn, she admonished him thus:

Now that the cock's up,
Just pull your socks up . . .

Our plans for Hamela included a passionate affair with Ophelia, whose madness was thereby averted. The girls were not to meet, though, and Hamela was never to knock her brother unconscious with a dildo – that dazzling *coup de théâtre* with which *Hamela* was supposed to end.

Some snatches of *Hamlet* have stayed with me – the soliloquies, Polonius's advice to Laertes, the gravedigger's talk of Yorick, among others. When I finally appeared in the tragedy I had spent a mad summer learning, I was given nothing to say. I was cast as a humble courtier, required only to bow and scrape, to move the furniture, and to listen.

SPUNK

Where had I read that this was the hour of the damned, when the tormented are startled out of quiet slumber? I remember asking myself that literary question as I lay awake in a state much like terror early one morning in my fifteenth year. I had just masturbated, in my brown-skinned idol's imagined embrace. Thoughts of pleasure were succeeded by feelings of shame and guilt. I sat up in bed, in the absolute darkness of the long hour that only ends with dawn, and realized I was among the lost.

Three years before, in pre-spunk times, I had known desire of the kind other boys knew. I could speak of it, if I wanted to, with the voice of experience. On that memorable Saturday evening, my parents told me I would have to sleep with the two girls who lived on the ground floor. My mother and father were having a party and some of the guests would be staying the night. There was no room for me upstairs.

'You can lie between us,' said the older girl, who was well into adolescence. I was under orders, and obeyed. She and her sister pulled back the bedclothes and made a space for me. In clean pyjamas, with my face freshly scrubbed, my teeth brushed and hair neatly combed, I had passed my mother's test for immaculacy: 'You've washed behind your ears, for once. Miracles will never cease.'

I wonder, now, who were the more innocent – the four trusting parents, or their three apparently guileless children. Into the bed I went, with no anticipation of the bliss that was to ensue. I had been instructed to go off to sleep as quickly as possible, and, when the girls' mother wished us sweet dreams and turned out the light, I closed my eyes and kept them closed.

They opened, in surprise, when the older girl guided my right hand to her large, round breasts, which seemed to grow larger and rounder at the touch. I was soon aware that one hand was insufficient to cope with the abundance of flesh I was being offered. She pushed me aside, asked me to wait a minute, and then made her nightdress ride up until it was like a vast collar round her throat. I had complete access to the swollen beauties, and pressed and squeezed them while she whispered that I should try to be more gentle and not be so rough. She then commanded me to kiss her nipples, which I did. From kissing I progressed to sucking and licking. In the meantime, the younger sister, determined to join in the fun, had lowered my pyjama trousers from the rear and now held my throbbing penis in a firm grip. It was still in her possession when I had the first 'moment' – for such was the name I gave it – of my life. I trembled with delicious excitement as it happened. At the age of eleven, I was too young to leave incriminating stains on the sheet.

*

'Semen' and 'sperm' were unknown words to us. It was 'spunk' we talked of, in and out of class. The more extroverted boys held competitions in the lavatories to see who could produce most and who could send it flying farthest. We were spunk-obsessed, in our differing ways, in the spring of 1950. The sticky stuff had us in its thrall.

'You're getting through rather a lot of handkerchiefs,' observed my suspicious mother. 'Yet you don't seem to have the sniffles.'

There were not many advantages in being immaculate, but this was one of them. Every morning throughout my schooldays, my mother folded a clean handkerchief into the breast pocket of my blazer, above the arms and motto of the school's founder: 'Rather Deathe than False of Faythe.' I rarely had colds, thanks to my love of oranges, and seldom sneezed, but now I could use what she called the sniffles as the reason for the stiffened squares of cotton collecting under my pillow.

'You never took a hanky to bed with you before.'

Often, during the night, guessing that she was awake in the next room, I pretended to sneeze at the moment of ejaculation. Cunning and deceit can be born of guilt, I discovered.

There was a boy in our year, I recall, who knew neither shame nor deception. He masturbated whenever he needed to, and his need was limitless. His desk shook with him as orgasm was frantically achieved, and only subsided when he was calm again. As soon as the word went round that he was 'at it', we tried not to snigger and the master tried not to notice. One teacher, and one alone, was openly amused by the spectacle. This dapper man, who wore floppy bow-ties, taught chemistry. 'Today I shall communicate to the class the ideas of a certain Avogadro, who is not to be confused with a certain Ava Gardner. Those of you who wish to learn about the Italian physicist's work on gases will have pens and paper to the ready – with the exception, that is, of the single-minded student in your midst who would appear to be interested in more stimulating pursuits.' He looked at the boy, whose eyes had already glazed over. Shortly afterwards, when the boy let out a resounding gasp, he diverted from the subject of Avogadro for an instant and enquired if E – was 'better now'? E – replied that he was, thank you, sir. 'That's good,' said the teacher, and went on with the lesson.

It was always at the hour of the damned – the time when most people die – that I felt ashamed and miserable. I tried, with infrequent success, to curb the need to masturbate. Boys who indulged in self-abuse could expect fearsome manifestations of that indulgence in later life – blindness, hairy growths on the palms of the hands and complete loss of memory were but three of the promised signs.

How did I know this? We did not talk of sex at home, and, if anyone attempted to, my mother brought discussion to an abrupt halt with 'Go and wash your mouth out with carbolic soap' or 'I didn't bring you up to think filth'. My knowledge was a common one: it was in the air, it was all about us. At school, in religious instruction, we learned that God slew Onan, the son of Judah, for spilling the seed his father had ordered him to put into Tamar, the wife of his wicked brother, Er, whom God had also dispatched. I did not view this episode, then, as yet another example of God's customary perverseness – I simply understood, as I was meant to, that Onan had committed a terrible sin, for which he was duly punished.

Seed-spilling was bad for you, morally and physically, but doing what the men of Sodom wanted to do to the two angels who put up for the night at Lot's house was infinitely worse. We had to know that 'to know' in the Bible was not 'to know' as we knew it. When the young and old males of that soon-to-be-destroyed city (by God, of course) de-manded of Lot that he bring his visitors 'unto us, that we may know them', they had something more than a friendly handshake in mind. The scribe responsible for Chapter 19 of Genesis is annoyingly vague on the subject of the methods employed by Sodom's welcome committee, and our teacher emulated his vagueness. We had to read be-tween the lines.

My feelings of shame were founded on nonsense, on unexamined superstition. Yet they persisted long after I had sent God packing. I continued to believe that I was unnatural, though a healthy strain of arrogance in me occasionally translated this as 'different'. That I wasn't really ashamed of being a coward and a hypocrite is what shames me, in retrospect, for I never rose to the defence of my fellow pansies when they were insulted or mocked. I stayed silent when I should have spoken, and was even a party to the mockery.

Two events, both comic in essence, signalled the beginning of the end of shame. In the first, a congenial young woman with whom I was endeavouring to make love on a friend's divan suddenly began to giggle. I persevered. 'What's the matter?' I asked, when her giggling became uncontrollable. 'You are,' she answered, pushing me off. 'You're the matter. You're soft where you shouldn't be. You want a man, don't you?'

'Yes,' I astonished myself by admitting.

'So do I,' she said, without malice. 'Let's go and get drunk.'

Her honesty and kindliness were beneficial to me, and we remained friends for years. In the second deciding event, it was I who laughed – inwardly. I had gone to bed with an actor who had converted to Roman Catholicism in his twenties. His tiny flat, at the top of a huge Victorian house, was decorated with icons. We had eaten a sparse dinner, which he had made sure we had washed down with a surfeit of red wine. Incense was burning in the bedroom when we undressed, in the dark. He did not care for kissing, he told me. What *did* he care for? 'Playing,' he revealed. The play, when it took place, was not inventive. My hand having fulfilled its required duty, he moaned and turned away from me. I pretended to doze off. Some time later, when he felt certain that I was asleep, he left the bed, stealthily. Then I heard him muttering, and made out the words 'forgive me', which he repeated. I opened my eyes and saw him on his knees before a crucifix. He was begging forgiveness – from Jesus, from the Virgin Mary – for wasting his seed.

In the morning, when he invited me to play again, I said, truthfully, that I was not in the mood. He demanded a reason. 'I'm just not in the mood,' I replied.

'Try to be,' he pleaded.

'I can't. I honestly can't.'

He glowered at me as I put my clothes on. I said goodbye, and thanked him for the meal and the wine and the play. I could not thank him, then, for the gift of his abjectness, which helped to release me from mine.

'"That girl's got more spunk than any boy I've ever met"' – the sentence, encountered in a children's adventure story, caused me to stop and think. A girl, with spunk? The only spunk I was conscious of was the stuff I couldn't resist spilling, despite the example of slaughtered Onan. I consulted the *Oxford Dictionary* in the school library and was initially bewildered. Was the fictional girl a spark, a touchwood or tinder, a fungoid growth on a tree, a match or lucifer? The fifth definition made sense: 'Spirit, mettle; courage, pluck.' To have spunk is to have courage, I learned. This spunk is rarer, much rarer, than the other kinds, and it does not stain.

MARLON AND TAB AND ÉDOUARD

I never stoop'd so low, as they
Which on an eye, cheeke, lip, can prey . . .

I read, stooping low to admire the eyes, cheeks, lips, neck, shoulders, chest and arms – all that was gloriously visible – of Marlon Brando. I kept his treasured photograph, torn from a film magazine, in my Oxford edition of the poems of John Donne, where I knew it would be safe.

'O my America, my new-found land': whenever I opened Donne, it was to find Marlon, in his ripped T-shirt, glowering at me. How often I returned that smouldering look, and how often it transported me to a sleazy hotel room in the Deep South, where he was always waiting. 'Shut the door,' he would command, and then no more words were said. I closed that door behind me countless times (in my tiny bedroom overlooking the railway) in lust-dazed apprehension.

With Tab Hunter, my imagination leapt into the open air. No danger, no menace, no bottle of Bourbon, no cigarettes, no deck of cards – those Marlonic properties were all abandoned. There were palm trees now, and clear blue sky, and the vast Pacific ocean, out of which Tab would rise, head first, in his glistening blond beauty. My private version of *Saturday Island* was different in one crucial respect from the film I had twice sat through three times in succession. In the movie, Chicken Doogan, played by Tab, rescues a nurse, Linda Darnell, from a blazing shipwreck. There is an island on the horizon, which Chicken swims towards, the gasping nurse in his bronzed clutch. When they are safely ashore, they named the island Saturday, because that is the day of their survival.

In the public *Saturday Island*, all goes radiantly for the castaways – with Chicken building a home of sorts and spearing fish, and the nurse doing those essential feminine things like cooking and making clothes from leaves – until a plane crashes on the side of a nearby mountain, with its one-armed pilot, Donald Gray, on the verge of death. The nurse, being a nurse, nurses him back to health, and soon finds herself falling for him. The message is clear: there is more to loving than mere physical beauty, and a missing arm is of no matter to a girl who's smitten. The pilot and the nurse become lovers, leaving Chicken to ponder his cruel fate, for he had hoped to have made her Mrs Doogan in America, when the war was over.

In my *Saturday Island*, the ungrateful nurse and the noble airman had been obliterated. They were *persona non grata* in Paradise, which was where Tab and I belonged. I swam with him in the warm sea, and lay beside him under the stars, and welcomed thoughts of earthly bliss. I stayed in Paradise, on and off, for an entire winter, near to, but far from, the railway lines.

After Tab came Édouard Dermithe, in his role as the incestuous brother in Jean-Pierre Melville's film of Cocteau's *Les Enfants Terribles*. Here was another blond beast to adore, to the sublime accompaniment of Bach and Vivaldi on the soundtrack. This wasn't trash like *Saturday Island*, this was Art, with Cocteau's voice rising above the music: 'Les privilèges de la beauté sont immenses.' Oh, yes, I agreed, acknowledging what I felt, as a worshipper, to be true.

When I was thirteen and fourteen, Marlon and Tab and Édouard enjoyed those privileges. I stooped low to prey on their eyes and lips, as other boys stooped low – but openly, happily – to prey on Ava's and Lana's and Marilyn's.

THE PHOTOGRAPH

Who was this talking of the Pacific and the Mediterranean, of faraway ports where his ship had berthed? Who was the stranger my mother and sister were entertaining in the front room on a Thursday evening? Who on earth was he, to be so honoured?

My sister called to me to come in and meet Cliff.

I blushed when I shook hands with him.

'He's not usually this shy,' my mother explained as I tried not to be dazzled by Cliff's beauty. He had a film star's good looks – sleek black hair, dark brown eyes and perfect white teeth. It was obvious from the first sight of him that his entire body was suntanned.

'How do you do?' I croaked.

'I'm fine, thank you, Pete,' he said. 'I hope we'll be friends.'

Cliff went out with my sister for a few months only, and then disappeared.

'Where's Cliff?' I asked, in a studiedly casual voice.

'He's at sea, of course. He's in the Merchant Navy.'

Weeks later, I enquired again.

'He can't still be at sea. He has to come home sometimes.'

'Well, he hasn't. What's it to you where he is?'

I wanted to know, I answered, because I missed the money Cliff gave me to go away and enjoy myself while he was courting her in the front room. It was real money – pound notes, not coins. That's why I wanted to know when she would be seeing him. There was no other reason.

'He's gone off on a long voyage,' she said.

The voyage was to have no end, for he never returned. Early in their courtship, my sister had left her wallet on the front-room table. Besides money, it contained photographs – one of our father, and three of Cliff. In two of these, Cliff was standing on the deck of his ship, wearing nothing but swimming trunks. The snapshots were almost identical. My heart beat fast as I stole the slightly more revealing photograph and slipped it into the inside pocket of my blazer.

Late that night, I transferred it to the safest of my hiding places – the Oxford edition of Donne's poems. Cliff's likeness remained by 'Twicknam Garden' for seven years.

I heard my sister tell my mother that she had lost a photo of Cliff. 'It must have fallen out of my wallet.'

'I don't imagine the cat would have taken it.'

A short while ago, I confessed to my sister that I had stolen the photograph she thought she had lost. When her laughter subsided, she told me the truth about Cliff's long voyage.

'He was sent to prison for fifteen years.'

'Whatever for?'

'He had an argument with a man in a pub. They got into a fight, and Cliff went on hitting him until he was dead.'

Cliff had never shown her his violent side. What if they had married? It didn't bear thinking about.

ENDING IT

I was serious this time, I told my mother. I'd said it before, but now I really meant it. I was going to end it all.

'End all what?'

'My life,' I shrieked.

'I see,' she said. It was a Sunday, and she was sitting in an armchair in the front room, reading the lurid newspaper my father had always referred to as either the Barmaids' Bible or The Whores' Gazette. 'How are you going to end it all, then?'

'In the gas oven.'

'I see.'

I went into the kitchen. I picked up the cat from her

place near the fire, and put her out on the landing. I closed and locked the door behind me.

I removed the shelf from the oven and turned on the gas. I placed a cushion inside and rested my head on it.

The gas hissed, faintly.

I could hear my sister screaming. 'He means it, Mum. He's doing it, Mum. You've got to stop him.'

'Leave him be.'

'We can't leave him. He'll die. How can you be so cruel?'

'Oh, quite easily.'

My sister was weeping. 'Mum, we've got to get him out of there. He'll die. Can't you hear what I'm saying? He'll die.'

'No, he won't.'

'He will. He will.'

'Now stop creating and airyating.' (That word, 'airyating', was a favourite of my mother's. I never heard anyone else use it.) 'There's no call for airyating.'

'What do you mean? How can you?'

'I can play games, too,' said my mother.

'But he's not playing, Mum.'

'Just leave him be.'

Their voices fell to whispering. Minutes later, I heard laughter.

I had been so intent on listening to them, and was so furious with them for laughing at me, that I hadn't realized the hissing had stopped.

'It isn't funny,' I shouted.

'Open the door, Professor,' said my mother. 'There's no money in the meter. Gas has to be paid for, like everything else in this world.'

I did not open the door immediately.

That was the most serious of my serious attempts at ending it. The others were serious in intention, but not in performance. Once, when I threatened to throw myself into the Thames, my mother said, 'Wait a moment,' left the kitchen and returned with a towel, which she handed me. 'I'd take this if I were you. You might get wet.'

I stood on Albert Bridge for an hour or more, looking down at the water. I reminded myself that I had Hamlet to play, and Richard II. It was too early for drowning.

I crept upstairs that night. I ate the cold rice pudding she had made for me and drank a glass of milk.

In the morning, as I was washing, my mother said, 'Don't forget the bits the Thames missed.'

SNOBS

'If there's one type of person I can't abide,' said my mother, 'it's a snob. There's nobody in the world has the right to look down his nose at me.'

Boys who read too many books, she cautioned me, ended up as snobs.

'Why is that?'

'Because they get ideas.'

'What's wrong with ideas?'

'They go to people's heads.'

And the people whose heads they went to, she continued, began to think themselves better than others, which just showed you how ignorant clever people could be, if you really thought about it.

'That Shakespeare must have been a snob.'

'Why?'

'Because of all those funny, high-falutin words of his. You never ever hear them on sensible people's lips. I bet you he must have had trouble making himself understood.'

'If people ask you what your father does for a living, tell them he works for the council.' That was my mother's firm injunction. 'It's as near to the truth as makes no difference.'

'But everyone knows he's a dustman.'

'He's not a dustman. He's a roadsweeper.'

'He *is* a dustman, sometimes.'

'Well, anyway, everyone *doesn't* know.'

'Everyone around here does.'

'I'm not talking about the people around here. I'm talking about other people you'll meet, people who don't know the family.'

In December 1948, the injunction changed slightly.

'If people ask you what your father did for a living, tell them he worked for the council.'

'Are you ashamed of what he did?'

'Of course I'm not.'

'Then why are you asking me to tell a lie?'

'It isn't very much of a lie. It's as near to the truth as makes no difference.'

'Are you a snob, Mum?'

'Don't you ever let me hear you say that again. I may be many things, but a snob isn't one of them.'

My mother advised me to keep my distance from the gypsy family who lived down the road. I doubt if they were of Romany origin, but their thick black hair, dark eyes and unconstrained behaviour – the children ran barefoot for most of the year – caused them to be accounted gypsies. As such, they were looked down upon by the neighbours, who shared my mother's wary view of them.

(In March 1989, in Romania, I had occasion to

remember our 'gypsies'. I was standing outside a hotel in Bucharest, waiting for my interpreter, when I was approached by a gypsy child with outstretched hand. At the very moment I gave the girl a few coins, the interpreter appeared and instantly berated me. Gypsies – this woman of otherwise impeccable liberal opinions declared – were thieves, scoundrels and, worst of all, parasites. Her rage startled me, and for the rest of that day I recalled how I and the other children of 'respectable' families had been taught to think of gypsies. In London, in 1950, they were 'parasites'.)

'That front door of theirs is open day and night.'

I said to my mother that I could not understand what was wrong with their leaving the front door open.

'Anyone could walk in off the street. Any riff-raff. It's because they're more used to living in a caravan, in the middle of a field, I shouldn't wonder.'

Worse than the perpetually open door, however, was the fact that the gypsy family picked hops in Kent every summer. To go off hop-picking was a sign that you were desperate for money: it meant you were poorer than poor. We lived in *south* London, not the East End, and took our seaside holidays as a respite from work. Hop-pickers enjoyed no such respite. They were out of place, it was considered out of their earshot, among the respectably impoverished citizens of Battersea.

'I wouldn't be seen dead picking hops,' said my mother.
'Why is that?'

'Because it means you've got one foot in the workhouse. And besides, there's the company I'd be mixing with. The lowest of the low.'

Some years later, the first West Indians, the 'darkies', moved into the street, and the supposed gypsies soon achieved what they had been long denied – the status of being considered thoroughly white.

VIC AND PLATO

'You'll have a book in your hand when St Peter tries to shake it at the pearly gates,' said my mother. 'If it *is* upstairs you're going, afterwards.'

I had a book in my hand, as always, on the summer afternoon I met the student of philosophy.

'What's that you're reading?'

I looked up, and saw that my questioner was the conductor of the bus I had just boarded. He had blond hair, in tight curls, and pale-green eyes.

'Poetry,' I managed to answer.

'Don't go for poetry myself. Can't get on with it. All words and no ideas. You ever read Plato?'

'Not yet.'

He brought out from his pocket a copy of the Penguin edition of *The Symposium.*

'Been at it, off and on, for months. Trying to improve my mind. There's plenty of room up there for improvement.'

He took my fare and gave me a ticket. His hands, I saw, were black from taking money.

'What's your name?'

'Bailey.'

'No, no. Your name name.'

'Peter.'

'Mine's Victor. Vic to the world. That includes you.'

(Inclusion in Vic's world was a rare and wonderful honour for me. I wanted never to be excluded from it. As it was, my time in that radiant place lasted about six weeks.)

I walked miles away from home in order to make the return journey by bus. It had to be *the* bus, Vic's bus – no other would do. I remember waiting at a stop in Whitehall for nearly an hour until *his* bus came along. I had spurned three without him.

'Hullo, Pete.'

'Hullo, Vic.'

'What you been doing up West?'

'Wandering about.'

'Wandering about's bad for you. Shows a lack of purpose.'

(I'd had a purpose – a mad purpose – that day. It was impossible for me to tell Vic the real reason why I was 'up West': he would have been horrified, surely, to learn that I was far from home because I needed to be longer in his company; he might have accused me in front of the passengers of being a pansy-boy. So my brain dictated, while my eyes took in his handsomeness.)

'I went to the National Gallery,' I explained, hastily.

'I believe you, Pete. Even though you're blushing.'

I was alone on the top deck of Vic's bus for the first time. I sat in the back seat, impatient for his arrival, excited and apprehensive.

'What you reading?' he asked, sitting down beside me and putting his arm round my shoulders.

(What *was* I reading? In the light of Vic's unexpected affection, books – and the words within them – suddenly seemed of little importance to me. I can't recall if I flinched automatically from his touch. I had become accustomed to people keeping their emotional distance, and was a natural flincher. Vic's arm stayed firmly where it was welcome, though; where it would be welcome, I am certain I told myself, for ever.)

'You don't mind me doing this, do you?'

My heartfelt 'No' came out in a whisper.

'You're all nerves, Pete.'

'Yes,' I agreed.

'You're shaking. Calm down.'

He kissed me, then, very quickly, on my right ear, which tingled from the shock.

The bus stopped, and Vic withdrew his arm. 'Work to do,' he said, and left me alone on the now-magical back seat.

When Vic greeted me with 'All clear on top, Pete' I knew that we would soon be kissing and cuddling each other. Yet I have to record that his more frequent greeting was 'The chest hospital's full' which meant there were smokers on the upper deck.

I asked him, once, as we sat together on the back seat, if I could meet him somewhere. We could go to the theatre, or the pictures.

'That's not on, Pete. Sorry, but it's not on.'

I was desperate to know why, but was fearful of expressing my desperation.

'See you tomorrow. In the empty chest hospital, we hope.'

The day came, a Friday, when there was to be no tomorrow.

We weren't alone in the chest hospital, I remember, and I was not in the back seat.

'It's goodbye, I'm afraid,' said Vic.

'Goodbye?'

'That's the word, Pete. Pastures new, as one of them poets of yours said. The wife's father's offered me a job in his business, so we're moving to the country.'

I noticed what I hadn't noticed before, that he was wearing a wedding ring.

'Wish me luck among the sheep and cows.'

I wished him luck.

'Let's shake hands, Pete.'

We shook hands.

'Here's a present for you.' He gave me his copy of *The Symposium*. 'I've made a start on *The Republic*. Tough nut for a bloke like me to crack, but I'll persevere.'

'Thanks, Vic.'

He was occupied with passengers on the lower deck when I got off the bus. I waved to him, but he didn't see me.

'You're moodier and moonier than ever,' my mother said to me at dinner the next Sunday. 'Why are you off your food? What's the matter with you now?'

Vic was the matter, and Vic's unseen and hated wife, and Vic's wife's horrible father, and those pastures new which held no welcome for the boy whom Vic had beguiled. They were the matter.

I read Vic's *Symposium* years later, in a philosophical frame of mind.

THE MUSIC OF GORDON RIOTS

Every student of English history knows that the Gordon
Riots took place in London in 1780 as a result of Lord
George Gordon's attempts to repeal the Catholic Relief
Act passed by Parliament two years earlier. The riots
reached their climax on 'Black Wednesday', 7 June, with
the destruction of property belonging to Roman Catholic
merchants, businessmen and shopkeepers. More than two
hundred soldiers died in the three days of rioting, and
twenty-five of the 160 people brought to trial were publicly
hanged.

In 1953, when I was sitting the state examination in
history at ordinary level, I knew otherwise. I had learned,
months before, that I had been accepted by the drama
school, and also that I was to receive a scholarship which
would cover the whole three-year course. My immediate
future was settled, secure. What did history matter to me
now? Why should I bother with dusty old facts when I had
so much that was new and exciting in store for me?

A demon answered these questions by putting into my
head the idea that I should write about a man called Gordon
Riots. I responded to 'What was the cause of the Gordon
Riots?' with the terse 'His parents'. Sensing that the exam-
iners might not be satisfied with a two-word essay, I decided
to elaborate. With further demonic assistance, I came up

with the notion that Gordon was an obscure eighteenth-century composer whose music needed to be reassessed. His most important work, I suggested, was a concertante for an unusual combination of solo instruments – Jew's harp, clavichord and musical saw. I was so pleased with this daft conceit that I drew five lines across the page, and filled the four spaces with crotchets and quavers. I hoped that it was clear from this brief example that Gordon Riots's was an unusual talent.

Why were Gordon's original compositions so little known? The clever-clever brat I was that day provided an explanation. Edinburgh, the prim and proper city of his birth, was partly to blame, for its citizens, even in musical circles, wanted nothing that wasn't familiar. The first performance of Gordon's Concerto for Three Bagpipes and Wind Ensemble was also its last. Indeed, the performance did not come to its rightful close, such was the commotion the piece inspired in the audience, who barraged the unfortunate players with oatcakes and whisky bottles.

In common with other pioneering geniuses, Gordon Riots was both ahead of his time and low on his luck. He should have had the forethought to change his name, and was often advised to do so, since the Scots saw red whenever a new work by Riots was announced in the public prints. 'I was born a Riots and a Riots I will die,' he declared proudly, to the annoyance and distress of his concerned admirers. Abandoned by his wife and children, he cut a sad figure as he shuffled along Princes Street, his head bursting with unwanted melody. It was hard being an innovator in that cold – cold in every sense – climate.

But Gordon was undaunted, and died pen in hand, the score of his newly completed opera, *Ossian*, on his knees. A pauper's grave awaited him, and a century and a half of obscurity. 'Poor Gordon Riots has yet to achieve the fame that is his due,' I concluded. 'It must surely come, if there is any justice.'

Then the bell went, and I realized that Gordon Riots's life and works had possessed me to the exclusion of the other topics on the paper. I left the hall elated, happy in my anarchy, convinced that I had failed with panache.

'You made a complete ass of yourself,' the history master said to me later. 'Why did you do it?'

I think I shrugged, and replied that I didn't know.

He persisted. 'Why did you write that nonsense?'

Oh, because it was fun, I lacked the courage to tell him – because I felt wonderfully free and irresponsible while I was writing it, unlike the rest of the boys, who were all scared of failure, all sick with worry. That was why.

I was tongue-tied, though, and incapable of defending my recklessness.

'Thoroughly stupid behaviour.'

His last words to me, on my last day at school, were warmer, kinder. 'That Concerto for Three Bagpipes, and what was it –?'

'Wind Ensemble, sir.'

'Wind Ensemble, yes. I should like to hear it. Perhaps I shall, if your friend Riots gets his due.'

THE COST OF LIVING

'That cabbage you're not eating cost fourpence,' said my mother. 'And those potatoes weren't grown in the back yard.'

'You've given me too much.'

'You can't have too much cabbage. Greens are good for you, especially when they're that price.'

After my father's death, the Sunday dinner became the excuse for a lesson in thrift. The only way to avoid learning how much she had paid for the meat and vegetables was to eat everything she heaped on the plate. It was wisest to do this in silence, for any expression of delight inspired her to say, 'That beef ought to be tender, considering the damage it did to my purse,' or 'I'd expect the apple pie to be delicious. I had to part with ninepence, nine whole pence, for the apples.'

Food left uneaten on Sunday reappeared on Monday.

Discarded turnips and parsnips would sometimes come to the table again as late in the week as Wednesday, chopped up fine and sneaked into a stew. People who wasted not wanted not, she reminded us. We had to watch our pennies, if others didn't.

'I'll have some more carrots, Mum.'

'If you say please, you will.'

'Please.'

'They set me back threepence, they did. You never used to fancy carrots. What's brought on the sudden change?'

It was impossible to answer truthfully. Whenever I had refused carrots in the past, she had told me I was being a silly boy. 'If you eat them while you're young, you won't have need of glasses when you're grown-up. They're good for the eyes.' Now that I was a regular masturbator, I chose to believe this old wives' tale. By consuming plenty of carrots, I could – perhaps – avert the threatened blindness. 'I've decided I like the taste.'

'Then you've come to your senses, and not before time.'

'There's nothing in this world that doesn't have its price, and what you can't afford, you can't have': these sentiments formed the basis of my mother's litany. Money – the use and misuse of it – was her constant theme. 'You'll die in the workhouse if you're not careful,' she would warn me, regardless of the fact that the institution, a feature of English life for 250 years, had been consigned to history.

My mother's workhouse was the same fearsome building her parents had conjured up for their children's benefit, and it had never been demolished. It stood in her imagination as the symbol of an ultimate disgrace. Behind its bleak façade, the paupers of another age toiled on for their daily bowl of watery soup and crust of stale bread, unchanged and unchanging reminders of the fate in store for the likes of those who hadn't counted their pennies. 'Once you're inside, you have nothing except what you were born with, which is what you leave with, too. Your father used to call the workhouse "a large grave for the living". So just you remember.'

I remembered, and often in my childhood asked her why she talked of a place that simply wasn't there. Since it belonged to a time before my existence, why did she keep on mentioning it?

'Because.'

'Because what?'

'Because if you don't know the value of money, that's where you'll find yourself.'

How could I find myself in the workhouse, if the workhouse was no longer here for me to find myself in?

'It goes by a different name these days.'

'Which name is that?'

'Oh, stop pestering me with your questions. You'll have to discover it for yourself.'

*

'The day of your funeral is the most important day in your life.'

I laughed, and she told me not to be so wicked.

My mother began saving for her most important day three decades, at least, before it arrived. It was only the lowest of the low who couldn't rise to the cost of a proper send-off. God might strike at any time, and it was best to be prepared. She didn't want that one last worry hanging over her.

'I've never owed anyone anything, and I've never seen the inside of a pawn shop, which is more than some in this street can claim.'

She paid for her own coffin, and for the car in which it was taken to the crematorium, and for the cars that followed it. She paid for the church service, too, at which her favourite hymns were sung. She had long ago met these final demands on her hard-earned money, so had reason to be proud of herself on the most important day of her life. She had risen to the cost.

FOR QUEEN AND COUNTRY

'The Army will make a man of you,' my mother predicted. 'You'll soon change your ways when you reach eighteen.'

My 'ways' meant reading books, listening to classical music and, most peculiar of all, 'prancing about' on the stage. Soldiers had no time or need for such things, being more sensibly occupied.

'It's come,' she said to me one summer morning. 'It's come, at last.'

'What has?' I asked, my eyes still bleary with sleep.

'This has.' She handed me an official-looking envelope. '"On Her Majesty's Service", it says. You know what that means, don't you?'

'Do I?'

'Open it and see.'

I opened it, and saw.

'It's the Army, isn't it? It's your call-up, isn't it?'

'Yes, it is,' I said, although it wasn't exactly. I had to undergo a medical examination, at an address in Holborn, first. I might fail, I thought.

'You won't be able to argue with them, like you argue with me.'

*

My mother insisted that I should look immaculate on what she called the 'day of reckoning'.

In London, in 1955, the young met in coffee bars, where they drank, and lingered over, *cappuccino* and espresso, which were unexpectedly delicious to someone who up until then had known only coffee-and-chicory essence, a dark and sour-tasting liquid that came in slim bottles labelled either 'Bev' or 'Camp'. I was a *cappuccino* drinker usually, but on the afternoon of the day of reckoning, I consumed six espressos in rapid succession in a bar conveniently situated opposite the building in which I was about to be examined. I did this on the advice of a fellow student at drama school whose obviously flat flat feet had kept him out of the Army. He had told me that lots of strong black coffee, drunk quickly, would give me palpitations.

The man working the Gaggia shook his head in bewilderment as I demanded a fourth, a fifth, a sixth.

'I can't keep up with you. Are you trying to break a record? How many more will you want?'

'I think I've had enough.'

'I think you have, too. Are you feeling sick?'

'No,' I lied.

'It's your own stupid fault if you are.'

'Yes,' I agreed, stupidly.

*

I was so terrified that I would be found healthy that I did not understand what the doctor was saying to me.

'I asked you if you have ever had a serious illness,' he shouted.

I shall be deaf, I decided, in my fear. I shall pretend to be hard of hearing, for as long as this dreadful ordeal lasts.

Diphtheria, I told him; I'd had diphtheria when I was very young. And rheumatism ran in the family – my brother and sister had both suffered from it, and so had I. And I often wet my bed, I added – if wetting the bed could be counted as an illness.

'How often is often?'

'Twice a week,' I said. 'At least.'

I now wetted my bed once a month, at most, but the lie, I assured myself, was essentially true. I could still say, with confidence, that I was a bed-wetter.

'It used to be every night,' I explained.

'Is that the only trouble you have with your waterworks?'

'Yes,' I answered, wondering what other troubles I might have. 'Yes, that's all.'

The day was hot, and I had almost half a pint of scalding coffee inside me, and yet I shivered, I remember. I went on shivering, as though it were midwinter in that stuffy hall and my puny body exposed to wind and rain.

I flinched when the doctor first touched me.

'The nervous type. We meet plenty of those.'

He took my pulse, twice, and listened to my heartbeat. He frowned, and I had faint cause to hope.

(That afternoon, I did not think of my father, who had fought in a senseless war – at Passion Dale, as I'd heard him call the battlefield. I thought, instead, of the immediate prospect before me, which was composed of more personal horrors than those summoned up by trenches and shellfire. I could catch, already, the sound of mocking laughter at my bungling attempts to play the soldier, and the sound chilled me. I envisioned waking up early each morning in a crowded barracks, my skinniness the subject of constant ridicule. Two years of military service would mean that my Old Vic Hamlet or Richard II – I didn't care which – would be delayed by two years, and that was two years too many.)

The examination of the body I often considered a prison was over at last, and I was standing in front of a board of old men, who all seemed to be staring at me.

'Is there anything more you wish to tell us?' The question was put by the oldest, in a kindly manner.

I waited – for the necessary courage, which came to me, like my assumed deafness, out of fear of the future.

'I think I am homosexual,' I said. 'I think I have tendencies.'

'We've failed you, anyway,' the same man remarked. 'You say you *think* you're homosexual. Are you implying that you're not entirely sure?'

'Yes. I suppose so.'

'Would you be willing to see a specialist. A psychiatrist?'

'Yes, certainly,' I responded, with an enthusiasm that expressed gratitude for my release. 'Yes, I would.'

'You're looking pleased with yourself,' said the director of the drama school when I rushed into the rehearsal room early that evening. 'Catch your breath and tell us what happened.'

'I'm free,' I gasped. 'I don't have to do National Service.'

'And how did you achieve your freedom, you decadent creature?'

I relished the laughter of my fellow students.

'I gave a good performance, Mr Hudd.'

'Quite clearly, you did. Congratulations.'

'I'm ashamed of you,' said my mother. 'And you should feel ashamed as well.'

'Why?'

'Why? You ought to know why. It stands to reason. Whatever will people think?'

'Which people, Mum?'

'Everybody. The whole street. They'll think there's something wrong with you.'

'But they already think there's something wrong with me.'

'They'll think there's something worse wrong with you now.'

'Let them. I don't care what they think, if it makes them happy.'

'You're no son of mine any more.'

'Whose am I, then?'

'I'm glad your father's not here today, to be as ashamed of you as I am.'

(Would he have been ashamed of me, the father who had said 'I hope you'll never get to fight abroad'? He'd used the term 'cannon fodder' about himself and his mates; he'd talked, in snatches, of Passion Dale, which I knew now to be Passchendaele – would he have despised me for the cowardice my mother accused me of later that night? 'I've brought a coward into the world,' she observed, in her distress.)

'It's me who will have to hold her head up when people talk.'

A month after the day of reckoning that wasn't, I went to a hospital in Tooting to talk to the psychiatrist. My outward self was immaculate, as usual.

He's either shy or mad, I remember thinking half-way through the consultation. How has he contrived not to look at me? Why am I addressing my answers to a bald spot on the crown of his head?

'Do you masturbate?'

'Yes, Doctor.'

'Often? Once a day? Twice?'

'Sometimes more.'

'Do you have a picture in your mind when you masturb-ate?'

'Yes.'

'Of a particular person?'

'Yes.'

'Someone you know?'

'Yes, Doctor. A boy I was at school with. He has dark hair and brown skin and pimples on his chest.'

What was the significance of the pimples? he enquired, without raising his head.

'They never vanished. He's had them ever since I've known him.'

Were my masturbatory fantasies confined to this one particular young man?

'There are film stars, too,' I said. 'Marlon Brando, Tab Hunter.'

'No females?'

'No, Doctor.'

'Never?'

'Never.'

'You may go.'

'Thank you,' I said and stood up. I bent down, to get a glimpse of his face. He was too quick for me, though, and covered it with his hands.

I turned at the door, for a first, and final, look at him, but his hands were still concealing him from view.

*

'What did the – the man – say?'
   'The psychiatrist, Mum?'
   'Him. Yes.'
   'He asked me a lot of questions.'
   'What sort of questions?'
   'Private ones. About my mind.'
   'I hope you were polite to him.'
   'Of course I was.'
   'Did he notice how smart you were?'
   'Definitely.'
   'Does he want to see you again?'
   'No, he doesn't. Once was enough.'
Thank God for small mercies. I wasn't as daft as she thought I was, if the man's opinion could be trusted. She hadn't welcomed the idea of a son of hers paying regular visits to a psych – to a psych –
   'Psychiatrist.'
No, she hadn't welcomed the idea one little bit. That would really set all the tongues in the street wagging – the idea of her son having to pay regular visits to a man like him.

GOD

'Whatever is that you've got on your face?'

'It's called a beard.'

'I can see for myself it's a beard. What I'm asking is: what possessed you to go and grow it?'

Had I been honest, I would have said vanity. I had grown it to cover the scar from an operation for the removal of a tumour. 'I just felt like a change,' was the answer I gave. 'Now I don't need to shave every day.'

'Lazy is as lazy does. It's natural for a man to shave.'

At the age of thirty-six, when I should have attained something approaching wisdom, I was still rising to her bait.

'Why is it natural for a man to shave?'

'Because it is. Your father would never leave the house of a morning until he'd used his old cut-throat. Poor as he was, he always looked respectable.'

'And my having a beard isn't respectable?'

'Of course it isn't. I dread to think what goes on in that mind of yours, but I did bring you up to be clean in body, at least.'

'I'm not dirty, am I?'

'I wasn't saying you were. If you want to walk round with a food-trap on your chin, that's your concern, not mine.'

'God has one,' I said.

(Here I was, in middle age, responding to my mother's

taunting certainties as I had responded to them twenty years earlier. I found silence impossible to achieve. I could not ignore them, ever.)

'God has one what?'

'A beard. A food-trap.'

'How would you know?'

'He has a beard in all the pictures I've seen of Him.'

'That's no reason why you should have one as well. Anyway, He doesn't have to eat. He's above things like eating and drinking.'

'Jesus wasn't.'

'Jesus wasn't what?'

'Above eating and drinking. And he was bearded.'

'If He could have put his hand on a razor, I dare say He would have done. They most likely didn't have razors when Jesus Christ was alive. I wouldn't use Him as an excuse for not shaving if I was you.'

I insisted that God and Jesus had not been in my thoughts when I had taken the decision to grow a beard.

'Then why bother to mention them?'

'Because they're respectable.'

'You're not to mock. It's wicked.'

It seemed that, once again, I was unrespectable and unnatural. The obvious hairiness of the Holy Father and His Son was not to be accepted as convincing evidence in my favour.

*

'You'll find yourself crying out to God when your time's up, like millions have before you. You're all cowards at the end.'

Everyone became a believer on his death bed. It was a known fact: doctors and nurses had told her so. The really bad types made the worst racket – screaming and hollering and begging for mercy, because they'd left it too late to mend their ways.

'Oh, yes. It's easy to say you don't believe in God while you're hale and hearty. It's very easy indeed. But wait until you're old and sick and breathing your last gasp – it's a different story then. Oh, yes.'

How often she summoned up that terrible final scene for my benefit – as often, perhaps, as her own mother had summoned it up for hers. Those informative doctors and nurses must have been excessively long in the tooth, for they had passed on the same fearful knowledge to my grandmother when she was little. It was from her snuff-surrounded lips that I first heard what would happen to me if I led a wicked life. No amount of weeping and wailing on my death bed would save me from the burning coals the Devil was busy stoking at this very minute. I was about five when she issued this warning: 'You be a good boy and you'll come to no harm.'

'I don't understand,' said my mother, when I refused to accompany her to my grandmother's funeral. 'She was very fond of you.'

(Fond? I remembered with what fondness she had tried

to cure me of my unnatural habit of wetting the bed. She sprinkled pepper on the offending section of the sheet and then pushed my face into it. 'You won't do that again in a hurry,' she predicted, as I sneezed violently. The miracle cure, administered countless times, never worked. 'It's pepper for you in the morning,' she would threaten, 'if you don't pee in the pot like the rest of the family.')

'She's your own flesh and blood, after all,' my mother continued.

'That's not my fault.'

God would punish me for being so disrespectful to the dead. I was to mark her words. 'You're no son of mine,' she observed, getting into her best coat. 'People will notice when you're not at the graveside.'

On the evening before the 'day of reckoning', my mother paid a rare visit to St Mary's, our beautiful parish church beside the Thames. She needed to win God's support at this crucial time, and it was wisest to go straight to the source. Some prayers were more important than others and had to be said in their rightful place, in front of an altar. Tonight's was one such prayer. It was far too serious for the kitchen or the bedroom.

She prayed until her knees ached. She pleaded with God to help her 'just this once', and, if He did, she would ask nothing else of Him, she promised. Could He make sure that her younger son, whose feet seldom touched the ground on account of his head being stuffed with Shakespeare, was accepted for the Army tomorrow afternoon? He had it in His power. She would be eternally grateful.

The following day, when I came home in a state of happiness bordering on the ecstatic, I could not properly gauge the depth of her disappointment, since I knew nothing of the desperate request she had made of her God. His refusal to intercede was never discussed in my presence – from fear, perhaps, that I would be 'wicked' and mock her.

The church I knew and loved as a boy dated from 1775, when Battersea was a village. Another St Mary's had stood on the site for centuries – since the Norman Conquest, in fact, when William I presented it to the monks of Westminster Abbey. Rebuilding began in 1379, and continued at intervals until 1639, with the construction of the tower. In 1782, in what was virtually a brand new church, William Blake married Catherine Boucher, the daughter of a local market gardener. She signed the register with an 'X'.

It was there, in December 1952, that I took part in the school's Christmas service. I had won the Elocution Prize that year, reading from James Elroy Flecker's play *Hassan*, and as a result my voice ('Here comes The Voice,' I heard a boy say once as I hurried into class) was in demand. One November morning I read the Lesson, chosen by the Headmaster: verses 17 to 27 of the first chapter of the second book of Samuel, in which David laments the deaths of Saul and Jonathan. The beauty of the sentiments and the beauty of the language exhilarated and moved me, although I was clueless then as to why the 'daughters of the uncircumcised' should 'triumph'.

In St Mary's I read from Milton's sublime *On the Morning of Christ's Nativity*, delighting in the glorious words. Of God's existence, however, I was already in doubt, and the notion of original sin I found curiously warped and unappealing. I know now that my continuing godlessness has its origins in the pretty little churchyard around St Mary's, in a childish contemplation of tombstones. On a bright summer evening, I realized death meant not-being, for the fading names above the graves were of people who had gone from the living world. The realization chilled me, and went on doing so, until I read Hazlitt, who provided – and provides – a welcome thaw. 'There was a time when we were not: this gives us no concern – why, then, should it trouble us that a time will come when we shall cease to be?'

My mother did not scream or weep or wail on her death bed. She simply drifted away. And a friend whose hand I held in his life's last moment bade me farewell with the trace of a smile. And, recently, another dear friend's long agony ended mercifully, with a loss of consciousness.

At my mother's funeral service, in St Mary's, I read from

Cymbeline. I wanted to say my public goodbye to her with lovely words. As I spoke the lines:

> Fear no more the heat o' th' sun
> Nor the furious winter's rages,
> Thou thy worldly task hath done
> Home art gone and ta'en thy wages

I remembered how she had complained of my constant spouting of Shakespeare, whom she regarded as a snob. I could spout, now, without interruption, and in the certainty that I wasn't giving her a headache.

ON AND OFF THE BOARDS

In March 1989, in the fearful Romania of Nicolae Ceauşe-scu, I had occasion to recall my brief career in the theatre. I was dining late one evening in the Bucharest apartment of a young English woman, who had invited three of her friends to meet me: another young English woman, and two Romanians – a censored writer and an unemployed actor. A group of armed policemen, knowing that I was in the building, waited in the street. We kept them waiting into the small hours.

(In common with almost everyone I met, the men did not refer to their president by name. It was He and Him they spoke of. 'He says there are no homosexuals in Romania and we must believe him,' said the actor, a smile supplying the irony missing from his voice. We were convinced that there were microphones cunningly secreted in each room.)

I told them of my time at Stratford-on-Avon. 'You were in *Hamlet?*' the actor asked me excitedly. 'Yes, I suppose I was,' I replied. 'Loosely.' He looked mystified as his fiancée translated for him. What did I mean – *loosely?* I had nothing to say. I was a silent Courtier, then a silent Player, then a silent Courtier again. Some nights, I found it very hard not to laugh.

'You were laughing? In *Hamlet?* In a great tragedy?'

It didn't seem like a great tragedy the way we played it, I said: not with a Hamlet who chuckled to himself when chuckling was inappropriate; not with a Claudius who indicated that he was decadent by eating grapes in a roguish manner. Something was always going wrong in our ill-lit Elsinore – the Ghost making a frantic late entrance on to the battlements, dressed only in his underpants; Polonius habitually talking of a 'calm and farters' instead of a 'farm and carters'; the Prince informing the court assembled to watch 'The Mousetrap', 'This is one Nephew Anus, Lucy to the King.' The attendant lords and ladies were frequently diverted.

Soon after the opening night, our Hamlet disappeared to London. 'He's running away from his bad notices,' remarked a waspish member of the company – with some accuracy, for he had gone off to seek the advice or comfort of his doctor and his priest. They recommended that he take a short holiday abroad, to refresh his body and renew his spirit.

During his absence, there was mayhem in Denmark. The court viewed the upstart Prince, his understudy, with derision. They backed away from him instinctively, to avoid the spittle that cascaded from him whenever he spoke. The Players, who were required to sit at his feet, received an unwanted shower for six performances. In the third of these our watery sub-Hamlet temporarily lost his front teeth – all seven of them, on a plate. 'Speak the speech, I pray you, as I pronounced it to you, trippingly on the tongue,' he was saying. On the word 'tongue', his denture went flying into the air. Seconds later, it was deftly caught by the alert Player King, who obligingly wiped it with a large red handkerchief before returning it to the Prince. There was no response from the audience, who probably assumed that the episode was intended as a comment on the advanced state of dentistry in eleventh-century Scandinavia.

The understudy, who was cast as Fortinbras, had his own understudy, who now assumed that role. The eccentric young actor had the oddest voice I have ever heard. It sounded as if he were being strangled, so choked was the noise that emerged with reluctance from the back of his throat. No one could persuade him to move his lips when he had to say the very last word in *Hamlet*, the vowel of which always went missing – 'shoot', as he pronounced it, became 'sht'. To the Courtiers' and Soldiers' ears, this more resembled 'shit' than 'shoot'. His 'Go, bid the soldiers sht' ensured that the tragedy came to a close with its performers in a condition verging on hysteria. Even the shoulders of the corpses were heaving. Order, of a sort, was only restored with the reappearance of the fortified chuckler.

'Did you never speak at Stratford?' asked the bemused actor.

'Oh, yes. I gave my Dennis, and my Lovel.'

'Your *who*?'

'They are men of few words,' I explained. Dennis is one of Oliver's servants in *As You Like It*. He comes on in the first scene to announce the arrival of Charles the Wrestler, and then goes, never to return. Lord Lovel, in *Richard III*, is a slightly more substantial character. Although he is as laconic as Dennis, his purpose in the play is clearly defined. It is Lovel who brings to the King the terrible proof of the decapitation of Hastings:

Here is the head of that ignoble traitor,
The dangerous and unsuspected Hastings,

he asserts, smugly. At one memorable performance, on a hot June evening, Lovel's smugness eluded me. His words went, too. I stood on the stage, Hastings's head in hand, unable to speak. I stared in total desperation at the famous actor playing Richard. He stared back at me. Long minutes passed. Then he broke the silence by asking, cautiously:

Is that the head of that ignoble traitor,
The dangerous and unsuspected Hastings?

to which I responded with a relieved and enthusiastic 'Yes'.

I left the stage feeling shame and humiliation. I had learned *Hamlet* by heart, and here I was forgetting my two miserable lines.

'You wanted to play Hamlet?' the Romanian actor asked me.

'Of course I did. And Richard II, too. I chose Richard's closing soliloquy as my audition speech. I must have acted it a hundred times.'

Then something extraordinary happened. The young Romanian leapt from his chair, dimmed the lights, and put some sonorous music on the record player. He addressed me excitedly, while his girlfriend translated that Richard's soliloquy was *his* audition speech and that he would like to act it for me.

He gave a full-blooded interpretation. His Richard was no milksop, but a still-vibrant youth railing against the tyrant who had ousted him. He had pride and bearing. His despair was fiercely defiant. His was a Richard for Ceauşescu's Romania, for those armed policemen waiting in the street.

146

I was in tears when he spoke the final words. More anecdotes about my dismal time in the theatre seemed inappropriate. I wished him and the censored writer the unlikely good fortune, the freedom, they both craved.

The police watched us as we said our goodbyes outside the luxurious hotel – built for the benefit of faithful party workers and foreign visitors – where I was to spend my last night in Romania. Did the Securitate already have my theatrical reminiscences on tape, I wondered? If so, what would they make of a false-toothed Hamlet, spraying advice in the direction of a group of players, and a Fortinbras bidding his soldiers 'sht'? Where there is tyranny, the silliest stories have to be decoded – especially when they inspire laughter.

'If you had any sense,' said my mother, 'you'd stay put this time.'

I was working in London's most celebrated department store, Harrods, serving the kind of people she had been serving more than half her life.

'You have prospects there,' she added.

'What prospects?'

'You can never see what's staring you in the face. That's been your trouble since you were tiny. I'm talking about prospects of promotion. You could rise high in a place like that, with your brains and your voice. That's why I'm hoping you'll be sensible for once.'

I said I would stay put until another acting job came along.

'That's not what I mean by sense. They won't promote you if you keep coming and going.'

'I don't want them to promote me.'

'Well, you should want them to. A grown man of twenty-four ought to know what's right for him.'

'Twenty-three,' I corrected her. It was her habit, always, to add a year to my age. 'I do know what's right for me. Being an actor.'

'There's being an actor, and then there's being an actor, and you only get to be one in fits and starts.'

'I'll show you one day,' I shouted, reverting yet again to a phrase of childhood. 'I'll be famous, you'll see.'

Those little ducks whom she'd heard fart before made their usual ripples on the water.

It was impossible to tell her that I was no longer raw with ambition, no longer certain of my dormant greatness. I feared her predictable response: 'I knew from the start it would come to nothing. You could have saved yourself the effort.'

(My mother's knowledge did not encompass hope in the future. The past and the present were more than enough for a person to cope with, and what was on its way was bound to happen of its own accord. If she anticipated anything, it was trouble, in all its guises. 'Those who expect the worst are seldom disappointed.' At twenty-five, I was already deeply disappointed.)

Twelve years earlier, I had dreamed of scaling the highest reaches of the actor's art. Now I simply wanted work. I might yet become a master of the cameo, since my few successes at drama school, on the stage and in television, had been in small parts, some of them comic. Perhaps I would find my niche playing Cockney, and other, eccentrics – the lovable rogues who steal the scene.

Even that faint aspiration was to be thwarted. I remained at Harrods, selling newspapers and magazines, my skills as a miniaturist unwanted and unused. In my free hours, I wrote plays, only one of which was ever performed – on radio, in 1965. My mother listened to it, and deemed it 'peculiar'. 'I'm the last person to hear about anything you do,' she snapped. 'You could have told me you'd gone in for playwriting.'

And have you mock me? I almost answered. 'It's not important,' I said. 'I think I'll try and write another.'

I made my debut on the professional stage at Christmas 1952, when I was fifteen. An actor and producer who had studied at my school some years earlier had seen me as Henry IV and been impressed. Would I like a job during the holidays, playing his son, Baby Bear, in a children's show called *Buckie's Bears* at a repertory theatre in Surrey? Someone else was directing it, and I would probably have to audition for him. Did I have a speech ready? Yes, yes, I replied, hardly believing what I was hearing.

The director lived in a wealthy London borough, in a vast apartment. It was there, in his cluttered sitting-room, that I acted Richard II's final soliloquy in order to secure the roles of Baby Bear and Gnome. The parts were mine, he assured me as soon as I'd finished. I would be paid £2 a week once the show was on, and £1 a week for the rehearsals.

As Baby Bear I was required to sing and dance as well as act, and often felt near to suffocation in my heavy bear's costume. At one performance, on the evening after Christmas, Father Bear was completely drunk, and Mother Bear and I found ourselves moving him about the stage and saying the lines he had forgotten. 'Your Daddy *is* merry this evening,' said Mother Bear in a very loud voice, to cover up the obscene suggestions he was making to everybody in the cast. 'Buckie must have put something really strong in Daddy's tea. Naughty, naughty Buckie!' This additional material sent Father Bear into hysterics. 'What rubbish are you talking, you silly cow?' he shouted. 'Not silly *cow*, Daddy, silly *bear*, surely? Mummy's a silly *bear*! Oh, you *are* a confused Daddy!'

That was an enchanted time, and I was desolate when it ended and had to be a mere schoolboy again. I missed the company of actors, and their frivolous dressing-room gossip – the knowing references to Larry and Johnny G, to Ralphie and The Dame, to the Scottish Play that no one dared call *Macbeth*, for fear of disastrous consequences. I was homesick for that provincial theatre for months.

In my second term at drama school, I played Mercutio in *Romeo and Juliet*, in one scene. Although I spoke the verse well enough, my puny body was gawky and graceless, and I moved without elegance.

No one in authority saw me as I continued to see myself – as a *jeune premier*, made in the classical mould. I was soon to be cast as crazed professors and ancient eccentrics, despite the fact that I looked younger than my years. My very last part at the school was that of a mad inventor, wearing an Alpine hat and lederhosen, talking inspired nonsense in a chalet half-way up a mountain.

I left the school with my dream of playing Hamlet intact. I would show those teachers what I was capable of; I would surprise them yet. In September 1956, I went to work as an assistant stage manager at a theatre in Essex. The company put on a different play every week – dire light comedies alternating with dire thrillers. The actors often performed like zombies, so acute was the strain of learning the unlearnable. They wrote their lines on shirtcuffs, on newspapers they carried on to the stage, on the blotter that rested on the inevitable desk, on the backs of curtains, in books casually opened in leisurely moments. There were forgettable words wherever one looked.

On Thursday afternoons, between the matinée and the

evening performance, I accompanied the leading actress to a nearby café, where two elderly ladies provided dainty teas. Our sessions usually began with a long sigh from Elizabeth. 'Men,' she would say, in her darkest tones. 'Oh, men, men, men.' These men were handsome, married, in early middle age, and totally untrustworthy. 'One day I shall come to my senses, perhaps. Why, why do I always fall for absolute cads?' Unable to answer this question, I listened, and nodded my sympathy. 'If I ever write my autobiography, I shall call it *Time's Eunuch*. It's from Gerard Manley Hopkins,' she explained. 'For that's what I am. Especially here. In this awful *hole*.'

'I was not born for Comedy,' she announced one night in the wings. Her voice was at its most sepulchral. 'I detest this *froth*.'

A week later, she was happy and light-hearted, giving her All as a woman who goes berserk with an axe five minutes before the final curtain. Elizabeth yearned to be Cleopatra, Hedda, Lady Macbeth. 'They're *meaty*,' she remarked, tucking into a scone with strawberry jam and cream. 'They have fire and power. They don't squeak sweet nothings. They are' – she paused, anxious to find the right word – '*women*.'

By December, I was in another company, touring the Midlands. The first play I appeared in was *The Prisoner of Zenda*, in which the villain was interpreted by a fat man with a speech defect. ''Tis her bwother, wed-headed Wudolf of Wuwitania,' he declared, his eyes narrowed to suggest intrigue. As the Goat Boy, in *The Teahouse of the August Moon*, I was in charge of a real goat with troubled bowels who was warmly attracted to my feet. This was not the theatre of my adolescent imagining.

'You needn't have changed your name,' said my mother, when I observed, with as much nonchalance as I could muster, that my theatrical career was over.

'There was another Peter Bailey in the profession. I had to change it.'

'You can be your real self again now. You were born Peter, after all.'

I had had my chances, and failed. At Stratford, saying nothing in *Hamlet* and *Othello*, I would remember that, only three years earlier, I had taken a leading role in a new play, *The Sport of My Mad Mother*, at the Royal Court Theatre. It had confused and incensed most of the critics. I'd hoped to make my name in it.

I heard, recently, of an actor with a wordless part in a production of Shakespeare at the National Theatre. He was, it is said, frustrated and bored. At what was to be his farewell performance, he left the action and walked down to the footlights. He stopped, centre stage, and stared out at the audience. He stayed there for several minutes. The other actors tried to continue with the scene, while the courtier hogged the audience's attention. Then a stagehand came on, and gently persuaded the errant actor to leave quietly – which he did. His had been, appropriately, a silent protest.

'DADDY'

He was still with me when I awoke from a dream of him. He was standing at the foot of the bed, smiling down on the son he had not seen for nearly thirty years.

'Daddy,' I said.

I did not dare to believe that he would answer me. I waited, but no words came. He acknowledged that he was my father, my long-dead father, with a nod.

'Daddy,' I said again, relishing the word I had had no cause to relish for most of my life. 'Daddy, what are you doing here?'

(I assumed, madly, that he knew where I was: in the guest bedroom at 1541, 7th Street South, in Fargo, North Dakota. The house belonged to my new-found friends Hal and Alice – they called themselves, collectively, 'Halice' – who were spending the summer in Britain. Some days, I had only their ancient cat, Flipsy, for company. My principal household task was to put down bowls of beer for the slugs in the garden. It was Alice's conviction that the creatures died in an alcoholic ecstasy: 'Much kinder than crushing them underfoot.' Each morning, I had to dispose of scores of Budweisered corpses.)

I sat up in bed, to be closer to him. When I offered him my hands, he vanished.

'Daddy, please come back to me.'

That was twelve years ago, and I have not seen him since. There is now no reason for us to meet. On a hot night in July, in a country he never visited, he gave me his parting gift, the gift I had been denied one far-off November.

It was as if America had been eradicated, wiped out: in that large bed, capable of bearing two ample guests, I was in the London of my childhood, calling out for the father who had gone from me. I was a boy, once more, pleading in a boy's voice. I spoke no other word but 'Daddy', for no other word seemed necessary. I wanted nothing else but his return, and the certain comfort it would bring.

I sobbed until my boy's body ached, until the source of all my tears was dry.

The next morning, I was restored to America and manhood. I felt serene. I had accepted the gift of grief, and my acceptance, my complete acceptance, of it had released something in me of which I had been completely unaware

– and might have stayed so always. If I had laughed him out of my presence as a mere illusion, if I had turned from him and gone back to sleep, then that mysterious something – a nurtured coldness; an icicle of long formation – would be mine today. I welcomed him, though, in the precious minutes he was with me, and ensured myself a night of pain. My first thought was that his vanishing meant rejection, but, as the night progressed, I came to understand its true significance. He was dying a second time – just for me, to my lasting benefit.

I drank orange juice, made tea, and ate a boiled egg and toast. I bathed and dressed. I left food for the cat, and shook out crumbs from the tablecloth on the lawn near the martin-house. I dropped the sozzled slugs in the garbage, and refilled the bowls of beer. Then I set off to walk to the university, where I was teaching summer school.

I talked to my class that happy day about the wonderful poems of Cavafy, in which he celebrates past pleasures shared in 'shut, scented rooms'. As I was trying to convey my enthusiasm for them, it occurred to me that the grief I had recently borne had been almost sensual. My body glowed, I remember, for having been freed, and I was not at all distressed when I discovered that evening that my father's unexpected visitation had brought me my first crop of white hairs.

HANDS

'What time did you get up this morning?'

'The usual. Ready for the dawn chorus. I can't seem to break the habit, old as I am.'

Old as she was, she now slept during the day – for as long as an hour, perhaps, or as briefly as a few moments. Once, on that September afternoon, she fell asleep in the middle of a sentence – and never completed it, because when she awoke she talked of something different. 'These dreams I keep having, they're quite naughty. If there's life in the old girl yet, it's all going on inside her head.'

I had asked her, weeks earlier, what present she wanted for her eighty-ninth birthday. I had received the anticipated answer: 'Don't waste your money on me.' Then, after a pause, she said, 'I tell you what I want. Your soup. Your soup will do me very nicely.'

(In the last decade of her life, I was my mother's soup-maker, by appointment. I was always a welcome visitor when I arrived with the plastic boxes containing vichyssoise, mushroom and asparagus, celeriac, or cauliflower and fennel. I was her absolute hero if I brought the curried parsnip soup she enjoyed most: 'I could drink that one by the gallon.' When I told her that a great friend had invented it, she remarked, 'You should have more friends like her, then.')

The bringer-of-soup had done her bidding, and sat by her side while she talked, dozed, and talked again. I remembered the lunch I had cooked for her the previous spring, and how she had wept with happiness as she tasted, and savoured, the dessert I removed from the pretty Victorian jelly mould in which it had set. The lark had not tired of waiting that Sunday morning, for I had risen before him in order to prepare the Honeycomb Mould. The pudding is made with the juice and rind of lemons, with eggs, gelatine, sugar, cream and Guernsey milk. It has a cap of lemon jelly, and beneath that a band of opaque cream jelly, and a honeycombed spongey base. 'It's beautiful,' she said. 'If it's beautiful, why are you crying?' 'Oh, it's just that it's taken me back. To the nursery in the first big house I ever worked in. That's where I ate this, over seventy years ago.'

'You've not eaten it since?'

'No, not till today.'

'Why not?'

'Nobody's had the patience to make it, myself included.' She dabbed at her eyes with a napkin. 'I've lived through two wars. Only think. It's like I was in another world, eating this.'

Whenever she came out of sleep that afternoon she looked about her: 'To get my bearings.' She stared at me each time, as if I were an interloper. 'It's you,' she said eventually.

'Yes, it's me.'

'I keep expecting to see people who can't be here.'

'I know.'

She put out her hand, and I took it in mine. We sat together, pretending to be interested in a film on the television.

'The rubbish they show.'

'You could turn it off.'

'It's company.'

We stayed hand in hand for several minutes. Words had seldom united us, I thought; had divided us, even. Her words, my words, and – especially – the words of 'that snob, Shakespeare' had raised wall upon insurmountable wall between the two of us. She was beyond sarcasm now, hadn't the appetite for it, the alertness, the energy. Realizing this, I felt a sudden chill of despair, the chill of loss. I pressed her hand and she returned the pressure and it seemed that the walls of words at long last crumbled.

I carried the warmth of her hand away with me, and have it still. Was she aware that she was making her final, loving gesture? Perhaps, for later that week the cancer that was to end her life asserted itself and she needed to be drugged to bear the pain.

A CURIOUS READER

The young man was sitting by the bed nearest the door. I saw him as I entered the ward, but he did not see me. He was reading a book, with eyes blinded to the life about him.

I noticed, then, the pile of novels at his side: Tolstoy and Balzac, in translation; Dickens and George Eliot. Not for him, in his illness, the literature that is known as 'escapist', offering a temporary eradication of the painful here-and-now. Pip and Dorothea, Anna and Vautrin, would make uneasy company, even in health.

'Who is he?' I asked the friend I had come to visit.

He said he would tell me later, when we took a walk.

What my friend told me, in the corridor, was that the skinny young man in the next bed had only days to live. He was suffering from a rare kind of wasting disease, and the doctors were as perplexed as they were helpless to save him. He knew his fate. On one of the few occasions he had spoken – between books – he had answered a question my friend couldn't voice. 'I don't want any visitors. There's no point. I told them all not to come.'

(Going home from the hospital that evening, I recalled, with distaste, how I had once believed I would die young. I had had Keats in mind, and Mozart and Schubert, as well as those awesomely gifted musicians who perished, one

after another, in the 1950s – Dinu Lipatti, Kathleen Ferrier, Guido Cantelli, Ginette Neveu. 'He was cut off in his
brilliant prime,' I had my obituarist write, 'but his legendary
Hamlet and Richard II will long outlive him.'

I remembered, too, thanks to the youth with the books,
the icy fear of not-being I had experienced on learning, in
my late thirties, that the lump by my jaw was a tumour.
With panic came a feeling of displacement, as if I had
been removed from the ordinary world with its small but
sustaining concerns. Nowhere loomed.

And now here I was, on a crowded underground train,
ten years on, marvelling at the young man's need for the
complexities of great fiction at such a time, and hoping that
he would reach the end of the pile, at least, before his
anticipated darkness claimed him.)

My friend was released from hospital the following day, so
I saw no more of the curious reader, urgently turning the
pages of *Lost Illusions*. There was no point, he said, in
relatives and friends visiting him – 'I told them all not to
come' – and I cannot presume to imagine what he meant.
Yet I wondered then, and I wonder still, why he didn't
consider that last, urgent need of his short life to be
pointless, too. He might have stared at the wall; he might
have chatted, as the other patients chatted, of commonplace
things. He chose to read instead – furiously, hastily – and
to live, for a short while, among the undying. That, he

might have explained to me, had I been crass enough to ask, is the whole point, precisely.

REMEMBRANCE DAY

It was entirely accidental that we met again on Sunday 12 November 1989, the official day of remembrance for the dead of two world wars.

I had last seen her at our father's funeral, in November 1948. I had not known then that she was already a widow, her young husband having recently died of tuberculosis. I had believed my mother when she told me that Mollie (as she prefers to spell her name) had wanted to adopt me. I heard, now, that Mollie could not have afforded to look after me, even if she had wanted to – which she hadn't – since most of the little money she earned was used to pay sanatorium bills. She had never lived in the spacious house of my mother's imagining, and scoffed at the very notion of spaciousness. The dingy, the cramped, the drab, had been her lot until she was in her forties.

It was to be an afternoon of revelations. 'I have a sad story to tell you,' she announced, after we had re-introduced ourselves to one another and she had greeted my eldest niece, whose interest in our family's genealogy had led to the discovery that Mollie was living in Surrey with her second husband. 'Jack will be hearing some of it for the first time. I've always kept the saddest bits to myself, because they were too painful to talk about.'

Mollie was seven years old when her father returned from Flanders. He considered himself a fortunate man: he was alive, he was in good enough health, he had a wife and two children, and he had a secure job with Whitbread's brewery. So he thought as he made his way back to London. He learned, within days, that his secure job – which he had been assured would still be his when the war was over – no longer existed. A woman had been given the post, at much less than his former salary. He would have to look for work elsewhere. He did, and was to go on looking, in common with thousands of other soldiers, for many years.

'I asked the question that caused all the trouble,' said Mollie. 'It was "Where's Cousin Cecil?" and my mother didn't reply. "You don't have a Cousin Cecil," said our father, and I told him, "Yes, I do. He's just a baby." And that was how it started.'

An explanation was demanded, and then Esther admitted that Cecil was her child and that his father was a tram driver. Mollie would remember the *sound* of the row that followed, the volume of it. The marriage came to its noisy end that day, with Esther being dubbed a 'scarlet woman'.

Their embittered father took Laurence and Mollie to live with his sister, Daisy, and brother-in-law, Tom, who also had two children. They stayed in the tiny house for more than five years, almost wholly supported by Tom, who ran a welding business. The boys and girls were ordered to be seen and not heard, while the adults argued and raged, night after miserable night.

'My mother claimed that Dad never "created" – to use her word,' I interjected.

'Oh, he created. He had a terrible temper. The slightest, most trivial, things made him angry.'

During those years, Esther was not mentioned. Mollie was forbidden to see her or to talk about her. There was no such person in the world.

In 1932, when she was twenty-one, Mollie was working as a secretary in an office in south London. One morning, she was interrupted by a member of the staff with the message that her aunt was waiting downstairs. 'My aunt? What does *she* want?' Mollie wondered aloud. The woman she came face to face with in the reception room was not her aunt but the mother who had been cast aside fourteen years earlier. Mollie recognized her and instantly fainted. When she came to, her mother had vanished, to Mollie's lasting dismay. If she hadn't passed out, she might have recaptured Esther's love, become her friend. After all, Esther had traced her to the office, somehow. As it was, she must have interpreted Mollie's fainting as rejection – a final rejection, not to be invited or endured again.

'That was the last I saw of her.'

Mollie was a clever girl, and girls were not supposed to be clever. My mother, who left school when she was almost fourteen, could not understand why her stepdaughter, whom she resented, wished to stay on, as clever boys did. Mollie ought to be bringing much-needed money into the house, instead of wasting time with books.

After Mollie received a coveted scholarship that entitled her to two years of higher education, my mother's resentment increased. She was pregnant with her first child, and Mollie's presence and manner irritated her.

Mollie was seventeen when she decided to leave the home she hated. She made her escape when there was no one in the house. She packed a suitcase with her few blouses and skirts and underclothes and those of her books that would be most useful to her and left, for ever. She stayed with friends from college, found a job and then moved into lodgings, where she continued her studies, 'burning the midnight oil'.

'He made no attempt to find me or take me back.'

With a mother's love denied her, with a father who never forgot that she had asked the question about Cecil, with a husband who was diagnosed as being tubercular only months into their marriage, Mollie's early life was a sad affair, saddening to recall.

I thanked her for her recollections, and we settled down to tea. I was curious to find out what had happened to Laurence, who was a salesman of Persian carpets at the time of our father's death. 'He married not one, but two, religious fanatics,' she informed me. 'The first belonged to the Elim Tabernacle church, and they served lemonade at the wedding. The second, Esmé, was a Christadelphian. Both of them were barmy.'

Laurence had died suddenly, in his fifties, but poor Esmé had lingered on, wasting away from the dreadful congenital disease, Huntingdon's Chorea. Esmé's brother, on hearing that he was also afflicted, threw himself under a bus.

Late on that Remembrance Day, I thought of my half-sister's father, who did not seem like my own father at all. I tried to imagine the quiet old man I had watched playing bowls as the soldier he once was, coming home to London to find his young hopes of secure employment and familial happiness dashed.

Some madness in him, the expression of his raw despair, made it impossible for him to love the daughter of his first marriage as he was to love the daughter of his second. She had asked an innocent question, and every time he heard it in his head he accounted her his enemy.

So I supposed, as I sat alone in the dark. When I came to be born, by mistake, twenty-six years after Mollie, my father's despair was no longer raw and raging. It was muted now, to be glimpsed occasionally in his blue eyes. On another Remembrance Day, in a vanished foggy London, he had talked of the miserable mess of Flanders, the whole stupid waste of it. 'Heroes, my arse,' he'd said.

I wept, then, for both my parents. He had cursed Esther from his deathbed, while my mother held him in her restraining hands. The memory of that name on his lips must have come to her often in her long, devoted widowhood.